# Access to History

General Editor: Keith Randell

# Stuart Economy and Society

Nigel Heard

Hodder & Stoughton

A MEMBER OF THE HODDER HEADLINE GROUP

The cover illustration shows the painting *The Tichborne Dole* by Gillis van Tilborg (Courtesy of The Bridgeman Art Library).

*Some other titles in the series:*

**Tudor Economy and Society**                 ISBN 0 340 55519 X
Nigel Heard

**The Early Stuarts**                          ISBN 0 340 57510 7
Katherine Brice

**The Interregnum**                            ISBN 0 340 58207 3
Michael Lynch

**Elizabeth I: Religion and Foreign Affairs**  ISBN 0 340 55518 1
John Warren

**Elizabeth I and the Government of England**  ISBN 0 340 56547 0
Keith Randell

*British Library Cataloguing in Publication Data*

A catalogue for this book is
available from the British Library

ISBN 0-340-59703-8

First published 1995

Impression number   10  9  8  7  6  5  4  3  2  1
Year                1999  1998  1997  1996  1995

Typeset by Sempringham publishing services, Bedford
Printed in Great Britain for Hodder & Stoughton Educational, a division of Hodder Headline Plc, 338 Euston Road, London NW1 3BH by Page Bros (Norwich) Ltd

# Contents

Contents

# Preface

## To the general reader

Although the *Access to History* series has been designed with the needs of students studying the subject at higher examination levels very much in mind, it also has a great deal to offer the general reader. The main body of the text (i.e. ignoring the Study Guides at the ends of chapters) forms a readable and yet stimulating survey of a coherent topic as studied by historians. However, each author's aim has not merely been to provide a clear explanation of what happened in the past (to interest and inform): it has also been assumed that most readers wish to be stimulated into thinking further about the topic and to form opinions of their own about the significance of the events that are described and discussed (to be challenged). Thus, although no prior knowledge of the topic is expected on the reader's part, she or he is treated as an intelligent and thinking person throughout. The author tends to share ideas and possibilities with the reader, rather than passing on numbers of so-called 'historical truths'.

## To the student reader

There are many ways in which the series can be used by students studying History at a higher level. It will, therefore, be worthwhile thinking about your own study strategy before you start your work on this book. Obviously, your strategy will vary depending on the aim you have in mind, and the time for study that is available to you.

If, for example, you want to acquire a general overview of the topic in the shortest possible time, the following approach will probably be the most effective:

1 Read chapter 1 and think about its contents.
2 Read the 'Making notes' section at the end of chapter 2 and decide whether it is necessary for you to read this chapter.
3 If it is, read the chapter, stopping at each heading to note down the main points that have been made.
4 Repeat stage 2 (and stage 3 where appropriate) for all the other chapters.

If, however, your aim is to gain a thorough grasp of the topic, taking however much time is necessary to do so, you may benefit from carrying out the same procedure with each chapter, as follows:

1 Read the chapter as fast as you can, and preferably at one sitting.
2 Study the flow diagram at the end of the chapter, ensuring that you understand the general 'shape' of what you have just read.

Preface

3 Read the 'Making notes' section (and the 'Answering essay questions' section, if there is one) and decide what further work you need to do on the chapter. In particularly important sections of the book, this will involve reading the chapter a second time and stopping at each heading to think about (and to write a summary of) what you have just read.
4 Attempt the 'Source-based questions' section. It will sometimes be sufficient to think through your answers, but additional understanding will often be gained by forcing yourself to write them down.

When you have finished the main chapters of the book, study the 'Further Reading' section and decide what additional reading (if any) you will do on the topic.

This book has been designed to help make your studies both enjoyable and successful. If you can think of ways in which this could have been done more effectively, please write to tell me. In the meantime, I hope that you will gain greatly from your study of History.

Keith Randell

**Acknowledgements**

The Publishers would like to thank the following for permission to reproduce illustrations in this volume: *The Tichborne Dole* by Gillis van Tilborg, The Bridgeman Art Library - cover. By permission of the Syndics of Cambridge University Library p. 80 and p. 148; by permission of the Syndics of Cambridge University Library / Fitzwilliam Museum, Cambridge p. 114.

The Publishers would also like to thank the following for permission to reproduce copyright material: xx

# Introduction: The Debates over the Interpretation of Stuart Society and Economy and the English Civil War

## 1 The Background

Over the last 50 years intense research has greatly increased historians' knowledge and understanding of seventeenth-century England. Unfortunately this has not meant that there is any agreement about what happened. This suggests, quite correctly, that there is considerable debate and controversy over the interpretation of events. Such disagreement is not just between political, social, religious, economic and cultural historians, but is also among members of these broad schools of thought themselves. It is all the greater because there are disputes about whether events in England can be considered in isolation, or only in the context of what was thought to be happening in the British Isles as a whole and in the rest of Western Europe. A major reason for this huge amount of interest in Stuart England is the English Civil War. Not only has it attracted the attention of a large cross-section of historians, but it has also been the centre of fierce debates in its own right.

### a) Nineteenth-Century Whig Interpretations

Until the twentieth century events in seventeenth-century England were studied largely for their political, constitutional and religious importance. History was seen to have been made by 'great men' drawn from among the ruling elites, so little or no attention was paid to the lives of the bulk of the population. Before the First World War English history was still dominated by this Whig (see page 12) approach, particularly by the writing of G.M. Trevelyan, who followed the literary style popularised by his relative T.B. Macaulay in the mid-nineteenth century. Although Trevelyan did include aspects of social history, these were largely derived from literary sources and dealt with the lifestyles of the landed elites.

### b) Capitalism, the 'Rise of the Gentry' and the Marxist Approach

It was not until the 1920s that social and economic history began to emerge in England as disciplines in their own right. One of the pioneers in this development was R.H. Tawney who, although a Christian Socialist, is considered to have been influenced by the writings of Karl Marx and Max Weber, the early twentieth-century German sociologist. Weber had carried Marx's notion of capitalism developing out of feudalism a stage further by suggesting a close link between the emergence of Protestantism and the development of capitalism. In 1926 Tawney published *Religion and the Rise of Capitalism* in which he applied the idea of the relationship between capitalism and Protestantism to England. By 1941 he had carried the Marxist theory of the rise of a capitalistic bourgeoisie a stage further through his article *The Rise of the Gentry*. This suggested that in England the capitalistic bourgeoisie were the lesser nobility, or gentry, who rose to power in the sixteenth century at the expense of the Crown, the Church and the greater nobility through their entrepreneurial exploitation of their estates. At the same time Christopher Hill began to popularise in England the Marxist materialistic concept of history developed by Marx and Frederick Engels in the previous century. This approach stressed the importance of social and economic change in historical development. Class struggle was seen as the means of overthrowing the capitalistic system and private property, thus, eventually, achieving freedom from oppression for the labouring masses. The first stage of the process was the transition from feudalism to capitalism which was seen as taking place between the fifteenth and eighteenth centuries, and was to lead inevitably to the British Industrial Revolution of the nineteenth century. The English Civil War of the mid-seventeenth century was seen to be an essential part of this progression. It was considered that by the seventeenth century a new class of progressive landlords and commercial bourgeoisie had emerged which, through the House of Commons, overthrew the forces of feudalism represented by the Crown, Church and the conservative elements of the aristocracy. It was argued that this bourgeoisie victory in the Civil War made possible the establishment of capitalism in England and cleared the way for the Industrial Revolution.

## c) The Beginning of the Debates

These two approaches helped to establish social and economic history as disciplines in their own right in England. They also ensured that social and economic causation of the English Civil War became firmly established alongside traditional political, constitutional and religious explanations. However, it was not until the 1950s, after the Second World War, that the debates on the nature of both social and economic change in seventeenth-century England and the causes of the Civil War began. It was from this point that historians began to engage in what has been described as a very fast game of ping-pong in which the rules were constantly changing. Many theories have been put forward since the mid-1940s to try to explain what have been seen as the unique social and economic developments in England which were to lead to the first Industrial Revolution. Until recently these general and other theories were based mainly on the notion that what was happening in England was revolutionary, and so controversy over what was taking place in the Stuart economy and society was scarcely distinguishable from the debate over the causes of the English Civil War. Although historians are still fascinated by both these issues, events now tend to be described as being evolutionary rather than revolutionary. A consequence of this shift of opinion is that it has become unfashionable to seek social and economic causes for the Civil War, or to see the Civil War as having a significant impact on the Stuart economy and society. In order to understand why and how opinions have changed it is necessary to examine the major developments in the interpretation of English early modern society and economy, and then to look in more detail at the debate over the social and economic causes of the Civil War.

## 2 From General Theory and Revolution to Diversity and Evolution

When the debate on social and economic change in early modern England began in earnest in the 1950s a number of clear guidelines had already been established. The nature of change was seen within a broadly Marxist framework of a movement away from feudalism to capitalism with the Civil War marking a significant turning point on the road to the Industrial Revolution. In Marxist terms this transition was seen as having been achieved through the progressive elements of landed and urban society overthrowing the reactionary, feudalistic old guard in the Civil War, thus enabling the successful growth of capitalism in England. At the same time Tawney's alternative theory of the rising gentry gained support when Lawrence Stone advanced the first of his theories of a declining aristocracy.

### a) Revisionist Re-interpretations of Whig History

At the same time other historians still preferred to see events in the early modern period more in terms of political and constitutional change, and began to modify the nineteenth-century Whig interpretations. This revisionist (see page 14) approach was to become one of the major counterbalances to Marxist general theories. In 1953 Hugh Trevor-Roper launched a stinging attack on the ideas of both Tawney and Stone in *The Gentry 1540-1640*. He criticised their methods and their conclusions and put forward an alternative theory. This proposed that while the yeomen, (large-scale farmers below the rank of gentry) rose, a majority of 'mere' (lesser) gentry actually declined. The only gentry who were seen to be rising were those who gained from royal patronage, or through the legal profession or commerce. This process was linked to the idea of the development of the state in the form of what was termed the Renaissance court. Trevor-Roper suggested that the growing instability throughout Western Europe at the beginning of the seventeenth century was linked to a conflict of interests between the smaller landowners, or 'country party', and the 'court party' enjoying royal favour. In the following year the Marxist Eric Hobsbawm in an article *The General Crisis of the European Economy in the Seventeenth Century*, put forward a different theory to account for this instability. He suggested that the breakdown of feudalism in the fourteenth century had allowed the development of capitalism in Western Europe. However, because the population largely consisted of self-sufficient peasants, who purchased very little from the markets, there was a chronic lack of demand which discouraged entrepreneurs from making investment in the economy. This he considered to be the 'crisis of capitalism' which would be ended only by the removal of the peasantry (the feudal cocoon) from the land.

## b) The Establishment of 'Revolutionary' General Theories

There was widespread criticism of all these various interpretations on the grounds of poor definition and lack of any real evidence to support them. A major critic of Tawney, Hill and Trevor-Roper was the American historian, J.H. Hexter who, in *Reappraisals in History* (1964), attacked them for using meaningless labels such as capitalism, feudalism and peasantry and for failing to support their theories with evidence. In his turn Hexter put forward his own theory that the military power of the English aristocracy had declined so that they had lost control over the greater gentry. This meant that political power had passed from the House of Lords to the House of Commons which, because of the resultant social and political instability, fought the Civil War to protect traditional values, religion and the constitution. At this point most historians retreated to the recently opened county record offices to find the evidence to support their theories. Even at this stage many of the central features of the ensuing debate over social and economic change were in place. The rival Marxist and revisionist schools of thought were established. The transition from feudalism to capitalism had become a key theory for support or criticism. It was widely acknowledge that explanations of what was happening had to be sought from long-term causation. It was also clear that the 'rise' of the gentry and 'decline' of the aristocracy were crucial elements in the controversy. Above all, these events were seen as revolutionary and the Civil War was considered to have marked a critical turning-point. During the 1960s and 1970s the application of the theories of revolution to sixteenth- and seventeenth-century England was very much in vogue. The search was on to discover why England, a backward military, political and economic country in 1500, emerged as the most powerful naval, political and economic nation in the eighteenth century. A leading figure in promoting the revolutionary explanation of the change was Hill. His *Century of Revolution* in 1961 was followed by a number books linking the revolutionary nature of Puritanism and the importance of intellectual ideas to the successful establishment of bourgeois attitudes during and after the Civil War. He saw the Civil War as the final removal of the 'dead hand' of the Church and the end of the Middle Ages. Such views were hotly contested by revisionist historians, but he was supported in varying degrees by other historians who saw religion as a vital factor in the process of social and economic change. The Levellers were seen as a strongly Protestant group promoting the social and economic aspirations of the 'middle class' sections of society. The True Levellers or Diggers - small groups drawn from the lower orders who set up their own communes during the late 1640s - were thought to be even more revolutionary. They were millenarianists, who saw the Civil War as presaging the second coming of Christ which would end private property and oppression from landlords and establish a perfect and just society. This theme was developed by Hill in *The World Turned Upside Down* in 1976 in which he saw popular social revolution being thwarted by the vested interests of the landed elites. The idea of revolution and the importance of the long-term social and economic causes and consequences of the Civil War had become firmly established.

## c) New Approaches

As well as the more revolutionary explanations of change other social and economic historians were developing a range of alternative explanations for what was happening in the sixteenth and seventeenth centuries. Intensive research and the growing use of quantitative statistical methods broadened the historical outlook. At the same time historians began to adopt the techniques used by other disciplines such as the social sciences, geography and anthropology. The new areas of population studies, family history, historical geography and urban studies developed alongside the more traditional lines of historical investigation. This trend produced such books as Jack Goody, Joan Thirsk and E. Thompson (eds.) *Family and Inheritance,* 1976, and Peter Clark *The Early Modern Town,* 1976, which produces a range of new perspectives. Many, but no means all, of these lines of inquiry were set in the framework of long-term explanations of the establishment of capitalism in eighteenth-century England.

## d) Neo-Marxist Theories

Significant strides were made in creating alternative Marxist interpretations. The orthodox Marxist theory was established in its final form by

R. Brenner in his article *The agrarian roots of European capitalism* in 1982. This suggests that changes in agriculture and the new forms of social relationship that these created were the major force in the transition from feudalism to capitalism. The starting point of the transition is seen to be the fourteenth-century 'crisis of feudalism' caused by the 'over-surplus extraction' of the peasantry by the landowning elites - the king, the Church and the aristocracy. Previously, surplus wealth had been taken from the peasantry in the form of royal taxes, Church tithes and rent. By the fourteenth century rising costs and over-spending by the elites had forced them to raise taxes, tithes and rents to uneconomic levels causing revolts among the peasantry. In England, although the Peasants Revolt of 1381 failed, persistent peasant resistance brought reductions in tax, tithe and rent levels during the fifteenth century. For similar reasons landowners were forced to give up labour services, thereby freeing the peasantry from serfdom. However, during the sixteenth century the elites were able to use their political power to raise rents and so to force the peasantry to give up their smallholdings to work for wages on the estates of the increasingly capitalistic gentry and aristocracy. The peasantry thus became a landless proletariate which was to provide the labour force for the Industrial Revolution. This explanation sees the main revolutionary changes occurring at the end of the Middle Ages rather than in the seventeenth century.

Some Marxist historians consider industry to be more significant in the development of capitalism than agriculture. In 1981 P. Kriedte along with other Marxist historians in *Industrialisation before Industrialisation* developed the theory of proto-industrialisation. This interpretation proposes that the establishment of capitalism was based on the development of cottage industry and the putting-out system. It is suggested that in peasant societies there was always a certain amount of industrial activity, especially textile manufacture, which was carried out by peasant families in their cottages during slack times in the agricultural year. From the fourteenth century clothiers (capitalist entrepreneurs drawn from various sections of society) began to organise this peasant production. The clothier supplied the raw materials which were processed by the rural workers with their own hand tool in their own cottages and the finished product was marketed and sold by the clothier. This is seen as the real beginning of capitalist large-scale production for overseas markets as opposed to small-scale craft manufacturing for local sale. In England, it is maintained, the expansion of this style of processing in the eighteenth century led to the Industrial Revolution in the nineteenth century. Although interesting, this interpretation has been widely criticised by a variety of economic historians on the grounds that it failed to explain why some cottage industries developed into full industrialisation while others failed to make the transition.

An alternative Marxist explanation for the development of capitalism was advanced by I. Wallerstein in *The Modern World System* (1971). This sees the growth of overseas commerce and colonisation as crucial to modernisation. It is considered that the expansion of world trade originated from the emergence of 'core' economic states in the sixteenth and seventeenth centuries. The three 'core' states of England, France and Holland are seen as developing a different form of internal social-economic relationship from the rest of Western Europe. This was based on wage labour and Protestantism. In contrast, other previously economically important countries such as Italy, Spain and Portugal remained Catholic and still had feudal, peasant societies. Consequently, while the core states expanded these other countries went into economic decline. They became the 'semi-periphery' whose markets could be exploited by the advanced 'core' states. The newly emerging colonies are seen as the 'periphery' with economies based upon slavery. They provided the 'core' states with a source of cheap raw materials and markets for manufactured goods. Because of their superior economic strength England, Holland and France were able to exploit the Spanish and Portuguese colonies as well as their own. By the end of the seventeenth century rivalry between the 'core' states led to colonial naval wars the outcome of which was to see England emerge as the leading economic power in the eighteenth century.

## e) The Demographic Determinist Approach

While these neo-Marxist explanations of the revolution of modernisation were being developed, a completely different deterministic explanation of early modern economy and society had emerged. This was based on the research on parish registers, wills, inventories and other sources being undertaken by the Cambridge Group of historians, such as P. Laslett, R.S. Schofield and E.A. Wrigley, in their study of population change and family reconstruction. Changes in population level were seen to be the main determinant of social and economic change. The demographic model of historical change, unlike its Marxist counterpart, was not 'revolutionary', although it did evaluate change in terms of long-term causation. Laslett in *The World We Have Lost* (1971) could see no signs of revolution in seventeenth-century English society, and, instead, talked of gradual evolutionary changes lasting into the nineteenth century.

Like the Marxists, demographers attributed the beginnings of such changes to a crisis in the fourteenth century. In this case the crisis was created, not by a change in economic relationships, but by the dramatic population loss caused by the Black Death of 1349 and the ensuing bubonic plague cycle which continued in England until 1665. The population in England and Wales was seen to have increased steadily from the eleventh century reaching a peak of some six million by the end of the thirteenth century. At this point rising levels of population are considered to have outstripped available food supplies, and the result was a Malthusian crisis in the early fourteenth century. This idea derived from the writings of the nineteenth-century English clergyman, T.R. Malthus who considered that as population in pre-industrial countries rose at a geometrical rate as opposed to food production, which only increased arithmetically, unrestricted demographic growth would result in population exceeding available food supplies. The result, unless the population took preventive measures to limit reproduction, would be crop failures, famines, malnutrition and a sharp increase in the death rate. This is exactly what is thought to have happened in late thirteenth-century England, causing a drop in population during the early part of the next century. Then just as population was beginning to recover, the Black Death (which is not seen as a Malthusian check) reduced the population by one-third. Recurrent outbreaks of plague are thought to have reduced the population to about one and a half million by the 1460s.

The sharp decline in population is seen as creating a Malthusian 'paradise' for the lower orders: wages rose because of the shortage of labour, lack of tenants forced down rents and food prices fell. Moreover, landlords were forced to grant personal freedom and freedom from labour services to a formerly servile peasantry. Many of the erstwhile peasantry were able to rent more land and so become yeomen and prosperous husbandmen, while others, attracted by high wages gave up their smallholdings to become landless labourers. At the same time the deflationary conditions are seen to have adversely affected the great landowners; the Crown, Church and aristocracy. Faced by declining rents, rising wages and falling food prices, they were forced to lease out large parts of their estates on low rents and long leases of up to 99 years. The beneficiaries of this situation are considered to have been the yeomen and the smaller landowners, or gentry, who were able to increase their land holdings cheaply. This provides an alternative explanation of the rise of the gentry and yeomen, and the economic decline of the Crown, Church and aristocracy.

When the population began to recover in the sixteenth century the situation was reversed into one of inflation. The growing numbers of landless labourers suffered a severe loss of real income because of static wages and increasing food prices. While some smallholders were forced off the land by rising rents, the more prosperous husbandmen and yeomen benefited from the price rise. Many of them, along with the gentry, were cushioned against increased rents by the long-term leases acquired from the great landowners. This meant that the gentry and the yeomen continued to rise until the end of the sixteenth century. By the early seventeenth century when the leases had expired, the great landowners, particularly the aristocracy, had regained their economic supremacy. During this period of rising population England is thought to have avoided slipping back into Malthusian crises because of the improved farming methods adopted by the yeomen, gentry and some of the aristocracy. Indeed, it is claimed that when, by the 1650s, the rate of demographic increase started to slow down the standard of living among the lower orders actually began to improve, so giving them greater spending power.

## f) Theories of 'Crisis'

During the 1970s the concept of 'crisis' became as popular among historians as that of 'revolution'. Malthusian crises were seen to be a recurrent occurrence on the continent. Various explanations were given to account for the fourteenth-century crisis, as well as the crises of feudalism and capitalism. Already in 1967 Stone had revised his earlier work on the English nobility in *The Crisis of the Aristocracy*. His conclusions that the aristocracy were declining in prestige because of loss of military and economic power seemed to have been largely confirmed by the demographic explanation of change. Urban historians, notably P. Clark and P. Slack in *Crisis and Order in Towns 1500-1700* (1972), identified an urban crisis. They argued that the major cause of the problem was that mortality rates in towns exceeded the birth-rate. This meant that urban populations could only be maintained, let alone expand, through migration into them from the countryside. Consequently, during the fifteenth-century demographic loss they shrank in size. However, the rapid population expansion in the sixteenth century created even greater problems because of large numbers of migrants which the urban authorities found difficult to feed, house and employ. Revisionist historians began to see signs of political crisis in the British Isles, Spain, Portugal, Germany and the Netherlands. This was developed by, among others, G. Parker in *Europe in Crisis 1598-1648* (1979) into a theory of an early seventeenth-century European crisis embracing almost every aspect of human activity. However, the theory was seen to be flawed when it was demonstrated by Dutch historians that Holland, far from being in crisis, was enjoying great prosperity.

## g) Growing Doubts about the Application of General Theories

By the 1980s historians had begun to become uneasy about the application of general theories. Doubt was cast on the whole concept of the transition from feudalism to capitalism. In 1978 the historian and anthropologist A. Macfarlane published *The Origins of English Individualism* in which he questioned the historical and sociological thinking that had underpinned previously accepted concepts. His main conjecture was that it was mistaken to try to explain why England developed differently from the rest of Europe in the early modern period. He maintained that from 1250, and probably earlier, English society had always been different and that thirteenth-century English society was just as individualistic and capitalistic as it was in 1550 or 1750. In addition, he doubted whether England had ever had a feudalistic society in the continental meaning of the term. The conclusions he drew from this were that models drawn by both Marx and Weber were essentially mistaken, and that neither capitalism nor Protestantism could provide explanations for what happened in seventeenth-century England. Although these ideas were not entirely accepted by other historians, support for the transition to capitalism and the revolutionary nature of the beginnings of modernisation has now become much less pronounced.

## h) The Growing Realisation of Regional and Social Diversity

It has now become apparent that there was enormous diversity in early modern England. Joan Thirsk, who is regarded as one of the leading English social and economic historians on the seventeenth century, had already shown the existence of great regional diversity in *The Agrarian History of England and Wales* (1967). Her continued work on agriculture, regional development, rural industry, and the growth of a consumer society clearly demonstrates the extent of such differences. Regional variations are now seen not to be based on only one economic activity but also to depend on the underlying variety of social organisation. The ever growing number of local, urban and regional studies has confirmed the existence of great social and economic variations. This evidence has been strengthened by research into the county gentry, the family, and women's history. 'History from below' has revealed the extent of the diversity among the lower orders. At the same time research into popular culture has greatly increased the understanding of social inter-relationships in local communities.

Doubt has been cast upon many of the previously held assumptions. Local studies, such as those by A. Everitt on Kent and J.P. Evans on Norwich, do not seem to show much evidence of revolutionary social change. Other research, such as Manning's *The English People and the English Revolution* (1976), appears to indicate considerable middle-order discontent in both town and countryside. The work of K. Thomas and B. Reay has done much to reveal the nature of popular culture and the attitudes of the educated elites towards it. Research in women's history, such as M. Prior's *Women in English Society 1500-1800* (1985), or S. Easton's *Disorder and Discipline: Popular Culture from 1550 to the Present* (1987), has shown different aspects of the role of women in early modern society. D. Underdown in *Revel, Riot and Rebellion: Popular Politics and Culture* (1985) sees social change in terms of cultural conflict. Some elements of society in local communities are thought to have wished to maintain traditional values of paternalistic society, good neighbourliness and communal, ritualistic religion. Others, particularly among some of the gentry and middle orders, are seen as wishing to display their moral superiority by distancing themselves from their poorer, and unruly, neighbours. Such evidence of widespread diversity has made historians increasingly sceptical about the usefulness of applying general theories.

## i) Revolution or Evolution?

This has led to growing reservations about the revolutionary nature of the seventeenth-century economy and society. Such changes as occurred are now seen by many historians as taking place in a context of great continuity and very slow transition. However, there is more consensus about what was happening to the economy than about the nature of social change. The establishment of capitalism is seen as a slow, long-term process. Economic progress is no longer thought of in terms of sudden, revolutionary, quantum leaps, but more as being a very slow evolution. Such changes as took place were often almost imperceptible, and occurred in different places at different times. Thirsk recently summed-up the situation with respect to agriculture very well by suggesting that at some times between 1450 and 1750 some agricultural changes were occurring in some places. Such emphasis on the evolutionary nature of economic change has led to the suggestion that the process should be seen in terms of the 'long sixteenth century' and the 'long eighteenth century'. Changes in the sixteenth century are considered to have started in the middle of the fifteenth century, and the first 50 years of the seventeenth century are seen as a continuation of the sixteenth century. Another period of evolution is thought to have begun after 1650, which lasted until the middle of the nineteenth century when industrialisation had become firmly established.

The extent to which this idea can be applied to social change is more open to debate. Macfarlane has proposed that English society was little different in the eighteenth century to what it had been in the thirteenth century. J. Clark in *Revolution and Rebellion, State and Society in England in the Seventeenth and Eighteenth Centuries* (1986) suggests that England continued to have a traditional, ancient regime society based on landed status until the mid-nineteenth century. While not adopting such an extreme stance as this, many historians do see social change in terms of very slow evolution, with many traditional features lasting into the nineteenth century. There is scepticism about the revolutionary impact of cultural conflict and social polarisation. This approach has been described as Marxist historians trying to impose revolution on a seventeenth-century society where such a concept was unknown. Some historians have described early modern England as having a one-class society in which class conflict was impossible. Doubts have been expressed about the revolutionary nature of Puritanism and intellectual ideas. Recent research into a number of Puritan sects, such as the Quakers, has revealed some very radical writing often by women.

However, such evidence is frequently discounted on the grounds that these were minority groups on the fringes of society and were thus unrepresentative. Research into the theatre and the use of literary criticism has suggested that radical political and social ideas were being debated by men and women at various levels of society. These findings are similarly dismissed as not being based on acceptable historical evidence. Although much of this criticism comes from post-revisionist historians (see page 14), most social historians prefer to see Stuart society in terms of tradition and continuity rather than revolutionary change.

## 3 Social and Economic Causes of the English Civil War

Alongside the controversy over the nature of the Stuart economy and society there has existed a parallel debate over the English Civil War. This has been largely between revisionist historians, who see the Civil War as being based on political, religious and constitutional issues, and those historians, particularly Marxist, who seek to find social and economic explanations of the war. The revisionist school of thought is based upon attempts to restate (or revise) the nineteenth-century Whig theory of history. This had developed out of the Whig (Parliamentary) and Tory (Royalist) political debate over the Civil War during the late seventeenth and eighteenth centuries. The major exponent of this school of history was Macaulay, who had perfected the literary, flowing, narrative style characteristic of Whig historians. He considered that the Civil War was a progressive and significant watershed in English history, and that the war had been fought over long-term religious and political issues, and against royal absolutism in the defence of the legal system, property rights and individual freedom. In his view the Parliamentary victory had established England as the leading constitutional democracy, and secured religious freedom. The Whig historians considered that history was made by 'great men', so that the Civil War was seen as being fought among the ruling elites with the mass of the population taking no significant part.

### a) The Beginning of the Civil War Debates

Until after the Second World War this continued to be the orthodox interpretation of the Civil War. Then there was an upsurge in interest in Marxist and in economic and social explanations of revolution. At this stage Trevor-Roper, participating in the debate over the gentry (see page 3), was the only prominent protagonist of a revisionist view point. In his view the war was a conflict between the country elites and the parasitical and expensive court. He was attacked for lack of method and definition by political, Marxist and social historians alike. In 1969 P. Zagorin revised the court and country theory in *The Court and the Country: The Beginnings of the English Revolution.* He agreed that the war was an elitist struggle between court and country parties, but claimed that the court was the dynamic centre of change. He also rejected the idea of revolution and the Marxist and social explanations of the Civil War. Another leading revisionist historian, Conrad Russell, in the *Origins of the English Civil War* (1973), restated the constitutional and political + relig. causes of the conflict. At the same time he deplored the fashion of concentrating on social and economic explanations which obscured what he considered to be the real issue - government. Russell and other political historians developed a revisionist explanation of the Civil War. This rejected both the Whig and Marxist interpretations of the war as being inevitable and having long-term causes and consequences. The conflict was seen as being fought among the elites over political issues. /

Social and economic concerns were regarded as having no direct influence. Although it was agreed that there were long-standing administrative and financial problems which led to the collapse of government ('functional' breakdown) in the 1640s, they were not seen as the actual cause of the war. It was considered that there was broad religious and political agreement among the elites until the 1620s. This consensus was ended by the unpopular policies of Charles I and his ministers which led to opposition by the supporters of tradition to what they saw as radical change. It was these short-term issues that revisionist historians considered to have caused the war.

## b) The Social Causes of the Civil War

In *The Causes of the English Revolution 1529-1642* (1972) Stone re-examined the then current position on the long- and short-term causes of the war. Using a sociological model of long-term 'preconditions', short-term 'precipitants', and immediate 'triggers' he produced a very persuasive analysis of the situation. The major preconditions were identified as the absence of a paid royal bureaucracy and a standing army; the decline of the aristocracy and the rise of the gentry; the spread of Puritanism; and a lack of confidence in the integrity of ministers of state. Puritanism was regarded as a key influence because it provided cohesion and leadership to the opposition and gave moral justification for rebellion. Between 1629 and 1639 the three main precipitants were seen as Arminianism, which attacked the concept of predestination and tried to restore clerical privilege; ship money and the attempt to increase taxation; and the attempt to enforce tighter guild control over industry. Finally, the triggers were considered to be the Scottish rebellion of 1638, which led to financial breakdown; and the Irish rebellion of 1641. This all created a crisis of confidence which Stone called disequilibrium or multiple-disfunction with everything reacting with everything else to produce the collapse of government.

## c) New Revisionist Interpretations

Although this reconstruction was widely acclaimed, revisionist historians, particularly Zagorin in *Rebels and Rulers* (1982), still denied the importance of social and economic causation. He defended his interpretation of the Civil War and suggested that the War could be understood only if it was set in a Western European context because continental monarchies were facing similar problems in Germany, the Netherlands, France, Spain and Italy. This latter approach was to become part of the orthodox revisionist interpretation which was restated by Russell in *The Causes of the English Civil War* (1990). For revisionist historians the English Civil War became firmly established as part of the wider Western European crisis of 'multiple kingdoms'. The difficulties facing the Stuarts are attributed to the fact that they were ruling the diverse kingdoms of England, Scotland and Ireland. This is seen as placing them under the same pressures as the Habsburg rulers of polyglot empires on the continent. The English Civil War is seen as being an affair of high court politics brought about by short-term problems with Scotland in 1638 and Ireland in 1641. This post-revisionist interpretation is well analysed by A. Hughes in *The Causes of the English Civil War* (1991). The Western European courts are considered to have been dynamic and creative but facing a crisis because of the military revolution which had greatly increased the cost of warfare. In England financial weakness led to functional breakdown because of the expense of war in Scotland and Ireland.

Although post-revisionist historians recognise the importance of underlying, long-term social and economic change, they do not consider that it had any immediate effect on the war. English society is seen as being stable, hierarchical and deferential, not highly polarised and divisive. The lower orders are seen as being passive and unable to challenge the ruling elites. England is considered to have been ruled by consensus politics, which enabled the aristocracy, in alliance with the greater gentry, to control the court and the House of Commons. Equally, there is thought to have been broad agreement in religion, and Puritanism is no longer seen as an individualistic, revolutionary force. Puritans can be seen to have been an over-zealous minority who came to the fore only because of opposition to Arminianism. Indeed, because social and economic change is now seen to have been so evolutionary and diverse, post-revisionist historians maintain that the causes and consequences of the Civil War could have been only short-term and political.

## 4 A Watershed in Mid-Seventeenth-Century England?

Clearly the confidence among historians after the Second World War that the Civil War marked a decisive turning-point, a clear watershed, in

English history has now evaporated. In 1973 Russell was deploring the fashion to see everything in social and economic terms. By 1990 Hill, in *A Nation of Change and Novelty*, decried the current fashion of abolishing revolutions. Although he unrepentantly maintains that there was an English Revolution which turned the course of history, few other historians would now unreservedly support him. In his article, *The Bourgeois Revolution of Seventeenth Century England Revisited* (1985), Stone was much more cautious. However, he did suggest that the abolition of the Court of Wards and feudal taxation may have given property owners greater confidence to invest which might account for the improved economic performance after 1660. At present the diversity of conflicting evidence makes it difficult for historians to identify any clear causal connections for events before or after the Civil War.

---

**Making notes on** *'Introduction: Issues, Approaches and Interpretations'*

This is a historiographical introduction to show how views on the English Civil War and the Stuart economy and society have changed during the course of the twentieth century. It is important to remember that historians writing about the seventeenth century are all familiar with these debates and so it essential that you are also aware of all the fundamental issues. Section 1 discusses the original nineteenth-century Whig interpretations of history based on constitutional and religious issues. Note how in the early twentieth century two theories involving the rise of capitalism and its link with industrialisation were beginning to emerge, and how these theories were then used to put forward a new explanation: the 'rise of the gentry'. This was the real beginning of the debate. From the next section you should make careful notes about the rise of 'revolutionary' general theories from revisionists, neo-Marxists and demographers and how they used techniques from other disciplines. It is also important to decide why historians grew wary of general theories and why the concept of revolution was replaced by that of evolution. Section 3 examines Whig, revisionist, Marxist and other interpretations of the Civil War and how they have developed over time. It is important to make careful notes about these various shifts in opinion, and particularly about how they are used to evaluate economic and social change. The next section looks specifically at what are seen as the economic and social causes of the Civil War. You should particularly note why they are rejected by revisionist historians and decide whether the present 'fashionable' view that the Civil War had no social and economic causes or consequences is valid. The final section re-examines the question of whether the Civil War can still be regarded as a 'watershed'. In the light of the debates you should decide whether the Civil War was a crucial turning point for the Stuart economy and society.

# CHAPTER 2

# Population, Urban Change and the Standard of Living

## 1 The Problem of the Sources

Most historians agree that the second half of the seventeenth century, despite the great underlying continuity, was different in almost every respect from the sixteenth century. This is certainly the case as far as population trends and the standard of living are concerned. Broadly the century can be divided into two distinct sections. The period up to about the 1650s saw a continuation of the average population increase of some 0.5 per cent a year that had been characteristic from about 1500. Hence, in demographic terms, the first half of the century can be seen as being the last part of the 'long sixteenth century'. For the great mass of people this meant the prolonging of virtually static wages and the upward movement of prices and rents. Thereafter the rate of demographic increase dropped and population levels fell slightly and then remained relatively stable until well into the eighteenth century. The easing of population pressure ended the upward spiral of inflation, and the reduction in surplus labour forced up wages. Consequently, for those in employment real incomes rose, allowing a significant improvement in the standard of living. This simple picture, while being generally accepted, conceals the difficulties of interpreting sources which have been described as flawed and unsubstantiated. The analysis of population trends for the seventeenth century is just as controversial as for the remainder of the early modern period. A major reason for this is that the source material is still very sparse, of doubtful accuracy, and open to a variety of interpretations. This has led to continuing debate over whether mortality or fertility is the most important determinant of either long-term or short-term population fluctuations. In particular, over the last decade historians have recognised that marked differences between even neighbouring parishes make it very dangerous to generalise about national population patterns.

### a) Parish Registers

The major source for demographic analysis and family reconstruction is the parish registers for marriages, births and deaths. These registers, which were started in 1538, have survived more extensively from the seventeenth century than from the sixteenth century. However, their usefulness varies depending on the ability, inclination and accuracy of the clergy who were responsible for making the entries. This differed greatly between individuals and depended upon their levels of literacy and numeracy. As a result, in many cases it is difficult to tell whether an absence of recorded marriages, deaths or births is genuine or is just the result of a failure to make the necessary entries. Equally, any seemingly sudden increase may just have been the result of more efficient record keeping by a new incumbent.

In any case, like most historical sources, the registers were not kept for the purpose for which they are being used by modern historians. They were a record of the names of people who were born, married or buried in the parish, and of the date when the event took place. This means that parish registers often fail to contain the statistical information required for demographic and family reconstruction. Vital information, such as the gender and age of infants and young children, or the age and cause of death for adults, is frequently missing. When the data is present it is often less useful than it might be because, for example, ages were often entered in multiples of ten. Medical knowledge was still so rudimentary that even when a cause of death is given it is frequently impossible to identify the disease or ailment in question. These and other omissions make it extremely difficult to calculate levels of infant mortality or life expectation, and to differentiate between the sexes or types of epidemic. In terms of marriage and fertility, the existence of doubts over the accuracy of entries is equally disturbing. If all marriages and births were not recorded it is not possible to make calculations about age of marriage and frequency of births with confidence. Both of these are essential when making estimates of fertility.

Such problems are made worse by a number of other factors. Geographical mobility was tending to increase and it has been calculated that there was a turnover of at least 50 per cent of the population of a parish every 12 years. This makes it very difficult to trace individuals from birth to death as they could be born in one parish, marry in another, their children could be born in different places and they could die in yet another location. It is also impossible to know how many people chose not to be recorded in the registers. Marriage in church was not universally the norm among the lower orders, and it has been estimated that 5 per cent of marriages did not take place in a church, but this figure may well be an underestimate. This was particularly likely to be true in the large open parishes (see page 31) of the woodland, forest and fens where many vagrants and other migrants were settling illegally. In addition, the growth of religious Nonconformity during the seventeenth century, especially after the 1660s, meant that an increasing number of people from all levels of society were not entered in the official records of the Church of England. Although it is possible to trace some of these people through sources such as recusancy returns (listing Catholics who paid a fine not to attend Church of England services) or Quaker records, many Nonconformists cannot be tracked down in this way. Similarly, the major censuses of Church of England communicants in 1603 and

1676 can be misleading and difficult to make use of because of the problem of deciding whether people with similar names are those who are being traced.

## b) Other Types of Sources

There are a number of additional sources available to help to fill the gaps left by the parish registers. Taxation returns and muster certificates listing men capable of military service continue to be useful. However, most of them record only men between and ages of 16 and 60 and male heads of households, and so give very little information about women and children. The Hearth Tax, which was introduced in the 1660s, is more informative than the old Subsidy returns which by the seventeenth century only gave brief listings of landowners and the better-off rural and urban elites. This new tax was based on the number of hearths (fireplaces) in each house, and so every household in a parish was listed. Moreover, all the households exempt from payment because of poverty were also indicated. While giving firmer national figures for the number of households, the distribution of wealth, and levels of poverty, it should be remembered that the new tax returns were just as prone to evasion and poor recording as the old ones had been. For example, one person recorded as owning a house with three hearths, which indicates modest means and status, left a will and inventory showing that he was a yeoman living comfortably in a well furnished seven-roomed house with assets worth several hundred pounds. Wills and inventories (the record of the deceased's possessions and value) are very valuable for filling in gaps left by other sources. They can give details of wealth and status, size of houses, occupation, children, relatives and business associates. However, their survival rate is very patchy, and they are no help in tracing a large section of the population who were too poor to have possessions that were sufficiently valuable to bequeath.

## c) The Difficulties in Tracing the Migratory Sections of Society

If it is hard to locate the more settled sections of society it is even more difficult to trace the younger and more geographically mobile elements of the lower orders. Apart from the eldest son, most children of both sexes in poorer families (the majority) left home in their early teens and led a migratory existence until their mid-twenties as apprentices, servants or vagrants. The movement of vagrants and their place of origin can sometimes be found in court proceedings. Records of the London Livery Companies, guilds and surviving indentures (legal agreements of service or apprenticeship) are useful in finding some apprentices and servants. However, the great mass of servants in husbandry and industry served only one-year contracts and disappear from view as anonymous members of the various families they served until they married. Occasional town and parish censuses and surveys and listings in churchwarden account books are of little real help in tracing this very mobile element in society.

Another particular problem of the seventeenth century is that an increasing number of people were leaving England either temporarily or permanently to settle in the colonies. Many went as convicts and indentured servants and can be traced through the convict transportation records or through surviving indenture agreements. Even then it is very difficult to determine when or if they ever returned to England. Furthermore, large numbers of unrecorded soldiers and sailors and other settlers were migrating to and from the colonies and following the ever expanding trade routes all over the world. Given these problems, it is small wonder that historical demography is considered to be an imprecise and controversial science.

## d) Family Reconstruction

The most comprehensive analysis of demographic change in England was produced in 1981 when E.A. Wrigley and R.S. Schofield published *The Population History of England 1541-1871: a Reconstruction.* Since then other demographers have exhaustively tested and reworked their statistics, methodology and conclusions. Although misgivings have been expressed, Wrigley and Schofield's findings, with some modifications, are still generally accepted as representing as accurate an overall picture as could reasonably be expected. A major difficulty with the statistical analysis is that it relies on a comparatively small sample. It starts from the known demographic structure in 1871 which is then projected back in five-year stages to 1541. This reconstruction is based on 404 parishes chosen as being representative of the 10,000 parishes in England. Unfortunately, some areas such as the north of England and the West Country are under-represented, while counties such as Buckinghamshire provide an unjustifiably large part of the sample. Furthermore, because of the lack of consistent survival of the parish registers, the data for 1541, for example, is based on the evidence from only 45 parishes. However, the overall population statistics arrived at by this method are considered to be quite sound even by its critics. Indeed, they compare very solidly with the results derived from a detailed study of 13 parishes over the same period. It is therefore the case that, although some of the figures have been subsequently revised slightly upwards, most historians consider that Wrigley and Schofield's estimates of demographic trends from 1541 are relatively reliable.

## 2 Population Trends, 1541-1730

The estimated population of England in 1541 was 2.77 million and by 1556 it is thought to have risen to 3.16 million. The severe epidemics of the late 1550s actually reduced the population to 2.96 million by 1561. This was followed by a period of rapid growth and, despite the bad harvests of the 1590s, it is estimated that the population level had reached 4.11 million by 1601. Relatively quick demographic increase continued until 1656 when the population totalled 5.28 million. This marked the end of the long phase of expansion and by 1684 the population level had fallen back slightly to 4.87 million. Thereafter rates of growth were very slow reaching 5.10 million by 1701. It was not until the 1730s that the population is thought to have recovered to the levels of the 1650s. Recently revised figures suggest a population total of 3.02 million in 1541 rising to 5.50 million by 1730. Both these projections are lower than the estimation of 5,500,520 for the size of population in 1688 made by the late seventeenth-century statistician, surveyor and engineer Gregory King. All these figures will certainly undergo further revision in detail, but the general demographic trend for the seventeenth century is now firmly established. However, historians find it more difficult to explain the underlying variations in the pattern.

### a) The Food Supply

Between 1500 and 1750 the population is considered to have increased at an average of 0.5 per cent a year over the whole period. Within this general pattern the rate of increase was not even and there were short-term changes when growth was checked and population levels even fell. The most rapid period of demographic expansion was in the sixteenth century. Over the first half of the sixteenth century population is thought to have risen by an annual 1.0 per cent. Growth was halted by the epidemics of the late 1550s, but then resumed at a rate higher than 1.0 per cent a year until the 1590s. Expansion resumed until the mid-seventeenth century but at a slower rate. This was followed by a period of stagnation and slight population loss which lasted until the 1690s. A new phase of modest increase of some 0.5 per cent then lasted until the middle of the eighteenth century.

It is agreed that this quite complex picture cannot be explained in terms of subsistence crises. Indeed, by the seventeenth century - and probably well before - English agriculture was well able to supply sufficient food to feed the total population. It is true that there were runs of bad harvests and some dearth years when grain was twice as expensive as normal. The worst of these occurred in the sixteenth century, particularly from 1594 to 1597, but the period 1646 to 1661 saw ten bad harvests, and there was another run of poor harvests in the 1690s and from 1708 to 1710. The problems of the 1590s and the mid-seventeenth century dearths are generally attributed to heavy rainfall, and the adverse climatic conditions of the late seventeenth-century 'mini ice-age' account for the other failures. Population growth was scarcely checked by the difficulties of the 1590s and the other crop failures came at a time of slow growth and even stagnation. Furthermore, it is agreed that food shortages and distress were only localised and were often made worse by the adverse economic conditions that had caused widespread unemployment among textile workers (see page 24).

## b) The Problem of Explaining the Demographic Trend

It is now agreed that the mechanisms controlling population change in England are more complicated than a simple reaction to food supplies. Although the British Isles are seen as forming part of the general European demographic zone, there are thought to be considerable variations between the different countries. England is now considered to be different from all its neighbours in that its population was controlled by preventive restraints rather than by positive checks from food shortages or disease. Demographers define this situation as being one of homeostasis: people married earlier after population loss through epidemics or during periods of economic prosperity, and delayed marriage at times of economic depression in order to maintain their standard of living. However, this situation was affected by rates of mortality and fertility, marriage and inheritance customs, and migration patterns. Moreover, all these factors inter-reacted with each other causing marked regional and local variations. In any case, there were considerable differences between towns and countryside, and between the social elites and the lower orders. As a result, there is disagreement among historians over what was the major determinant of demographic change. The major debate is over whether seventeenth-century population trends were most affected by fertility rates or by mortality rates. There is also disagreement over the impact of urbanisation and migration and over the standard of living of the lower orders and its effects.

## 3 Disease and Mortality

There is general agreement that disease and epidemics could influence population levels both nationally and locally in the short term, but there is disagreement about their long-term effects. Although bubonic plague disappeared from England during the seventeenth century, it is thought that the number of killer diseases, such as cholera and smallpox, actually increased. Epidemics were almost endemic in towns, especially in very unhygienic poorer quarters. Medical knowledge and midwifery practice were improving only very slowly and life expectation from birth is considered to have been only about 35 years. Of course, this low figure results from the high levels of mortality among infants and children under the age of 10. It is thought that adults surviving to the age of 30 could well expect to live for another 20 to 30 years. As disease was so prevalent it has been maintained that it must have had a long-lasting influence on the population. Although this theory is still held, more historians are accepting the Cambridge Group's (see page 7) view that nationally losses through disease were quickly restored through increased fertility. This argues that mortality crises created greater opportunities for land and employment so that people could marry earlier which meant that they had more children and so increased the birth rate. Epidemics could have a lasting effect upon the population of some towns and localities, but their long-term influence on the population as a whole is seen as slight.

## a) Mortality Less Important in England than on the Continent

For this reason England is considered to be different from its neighbours where mortality rates are still thought to have been the major demographic influence. This difference has been explained in part by the fact that England had escaped the cycle of subsistence crises, with the consequence that famines were only localised. Although there is no direct link between disease and famine, (epidemics often occurred during runs of good harvests), the death rate from epidemics was higher during times of food shortages. This is not thought to have been important in England, but in the countries with more extensive and persistent famines dearth and malnutrition are considered to have had a much greater influence on the impact of disease. In contrast to the continent, England also escaped the worst horrors of prolonged warfare, such as the Thirty Years War, which caused widespread death, disease and depopulation. It is true that the Civil War did have a similar effect but on a much smaller scale. For example, the burial registers in Oxford show a marked rise in the number of mortalities while it was under siege. Another hazard was the fire in October 1644, reputedly started by a drunken soldier, which destroyed more than 300 houses. At the same time the neighbouring market town of Wantage had a serious outbreak of bubonic plague, and was reduced to 'dearth and destitution' after being attacked by the royalist army. However, the fighting in England was localised and of short duration, and seems to have had no lasting effect on population levels.

## b) The Continued Influence of Mortality on Population Levels

Although this is a persuasive argument, of course the influence of mortality cannot be entirely ruled out. For example, it is generally agreed that the rapid population increase of the sixteenth century can be attributed to the lessening effect of bubonic plague and other epidemics as compared with the late medieval period. Furthermore, population stagnation after 1650 can be seen to coincide with the increased virulence of diseases such as smallpox and the introduction of new diseases such as malaria. In any case the rapid demographic growth of the sixteenth century does not altogether fit into the theory of homeostasis because the worsening economic conditions should have resulted in a lower birth rate. A possible explanation of this apparent anomaly is that the increased employment opportunities offered by rural industry encouraged earlier marriage than would have been possible in a purely agricultural economy. On the other hand, it can be argued that employment prospects were even better in the late seventeenth century. This may indicate that mortality had a greater influence than is currently accepted.

Despite the eventual disappearance of bubonic plague, Stuart England, especially for town dwellers, was an unhealthy place to live. There were serious outbreaks of bubonic plague in 1603, 1625 and 1665-6. These were particularly bad in London, and it is estimated that about 33,000 people died in the capital in 1603 and more than twice that number in 1665-6. Other towns, such as Norwich, Plymouth and Bristol, were less affected, but it is thought that Leeds lost a third of its population in the epidemic in the West Riding of Yorkshire during the 1640s. The reason why bubonic plague died out in England after 1666 is not altogether clear. The disease may have become less virulent during the sixteenth century, or possibly resistance to infection was higher. It is certain that, for whatever reason, outbreaks became more spasmodic. Those that did occur were probably the result of re-introduction from the continent through London and other ports. It is thought that it was this re-introduction of new strains of existing infections from abroad, allied with the introduction of some new diseases, that increased levels of mortality during the seventeenth century. A major reason for this was the growth of world trade and shipping which meant that more people were leaving, returning to, and visiting England. This resulted in there being more potential carriers of disease. The major killer-diseases of the late seventeenth and early eighteenth centuries were influenza, typhoid, dysentery, measles, smallpox and malaria. For some, as yet unknown, reason these diseases, particularly smallpox, became very virulent in Stuart England. There were severe epidemics in the towns, especially in London, where smallpox was endemic. Although the countryside was generally healthier, the fens, marshes and river estuaries were extremely vulnerable to water-born infections, such as dysentery and malaria. The evidence of the parish registers during the seventeenth century shows burials beginning to exceed births.

For this reason some demographers consider that mortality must be seen as playing an important part in explaining the population pattern between 1650 and 1750. However, it can equally well be maintained that the rise in the ratio of deaths to baptisms resulted more from a drop in fertility rather than from a rise in mortality. At present this is a subject of dispute among historians. Furthermore, it is uncertain exactly how mortality fitted into the demographic and economic system, and what links it had with such things as marriage and food supply.

## c) The Influence of Fertility on Mortality

For most of the population levels of fertility depend very much on where an individual or family lived. This did not apply to the elites who expanded rapidly wherever they lived. Their greater wealth and higher standard of living enabled elite women to marry earlier and meant that fewer of their children were likely to die before reaching adulthood. Among other sections of society, those living in the countryside were likely to live longer and have more surviving children than those living in towns and industrial areas. However, the situation was more complicated than this suggests, because demographic growth was greater in towns and industrial areas than in the countryside. The reason for this was that that greater employment opportunities in those areas enabled people to marry earlier and have more children. In closed fielden parishes, where agriculture was virtually the only source of employment and access to land was limited, population tended to be more stable, but stagnating if not declining. This was because marriage was generally late and most younger children had to leave to settle and find work. On the other hand, more families stayed in the parish for several generations because of security of employment and the extra welfare offered by parish poor relief. The working families were generally poor because agricultural wages were lower than those for industry. However, they were not likely to be totally unemployed or to starve, and were less prone to disease because such parishes were unattractive to migrants. In contrast, open parishes offered a range of industrial and agricultural employment and easy access to land. This allowed earlier marriage and attracted migrants and so created expanding, volatile populations. On the other hand, these parishes offered much less security. Poor relief was very patchy in such areas, and a down-turn in the economy could cause widespread unemployment and destitution especially among textile workers.

---

Letter from the Privy Council to Justices of Clothmaking Counties, 1621-2

1 We do hereby require you to call before you such clothiers as you shall think fitting, and to deal effectively with them for the employment of such weavers, spinners and other persons as are

now out of work, where we may not omit to let you know, that as
5 we have employed our best endeavours in favour of the clothiers
both for the vent [sale] of their cloth and for moderation in the
price of wool (of which we hope they shall speedily find the effects),
so may we not endure that the clothiers in that or any other county |
should at their pleasure, dismiss their workfolks, who, being many
10 in number and most of them of the poorer sort, are in such cases
likely by their clamours to disturb the quiet government of those
parts wherein they live. And if there shall be found greater numbers |
of poor people than the clothiers can receive and employ , we think
it fit and accordingly require you to take order for putting the
15 statute [Poor Law] in execution, whereby there is provision made
in that behalf by raising of public stocks [materials] for the
employment of such in that trade as want work.

---

## d) High Mortality in Towns and Industrial Areas

Mortality from diseases carried by migrants or from the polluted and
hazardous working conditions was high. In the Midlands and the North
new towns, such as Birmingham, Wolverhampton, Bradford and
Manchester, were being created from the amalgamation of industrialised parishes. Overcrowding and lack of sanitation increased the danger
of serious epidemics, like those of the 1640s (see page 23). While some
of the older towns, such as Southampton, Chester and Lincoln, fell into
decay, those offering employment prospects and good poor relief were
very attractive to migrants. London alone had doubled its population by
1700, and it is calculated that this growth required an average of 8,000
migrants per year throughout the century. Similar, if less spectacular
expansion, was occurring in many other towns. As the number of deaths
exceeded births (0.87 births for every death in London) in the towns this
meant that very large numbers of young migrants were needed to
maintain such growth and this may well have reduced fertility in other
parts of the country (see page 34). Even more strikingly, because
migrants had no immunity large numbers died rapidly from the diseases
endemic in the towns. This, by reducing a potentially highly fertile
section of society, may have helped to cause the stagnation in national
population growth, and reduced the average life expectation from birth.

## e) The Overall Effect of Mortality

The short- and long-term influences of mortality are still not altogether
clear. It has been calculated that local populations could be reduced by
25 per cent over a three-year period by disease and food shortages.
Although there were great differences between parishes, it is thought
that such short-term population losses generally could be quickly

recovered through earlier marriage. However, the demographic impact of mortality in the longer term is less certain and it is not clear to what extent population stagnation after 1650 was due to a decrease in life expectation, and to what extent it was due to a reduction in the birth-rate. There were differences in mortality levels between age groups of children, and these changed over the course of the seventeenth century. The death rate among children under five increased, while it fell very slightly for those between five and ten. The reason for the rise in child deaths is thought to be their vulnerability to the new virulence of diseases, especially smallpox. Mortality was highest among first births, although the survival rate for births after the fifth was also poor. The children of poor families living in depressed urban parishes, such as the suburb of Stepney in the East End of London, were especially at risk, as were those living in unhealthy, marshy rural areas. The impact of child mortality on life expectation is very marked. Having attained adulthood men and women from all social groups could expect to live until the age of 58, more than 20 years longer than life expectation from birth.

The major problem (as yet not resolved by demographers) is to decide whether mortality, which was largely the result of disease, was a major determinant of population level. It is thought that seventeenth-century homeostatis gave England a coherent population system based on social, economic, cultural and environmental circumstances. If this was the case, disease, which is exogenous (a random external factor), was not linked strongly to social and economic change, and could only have been a variable within the system.

## 4 Marriage, the Family and Fertility

If homeostatis did exist in England, fertility would have a more important impact on population levels than mortality. Nuptiality is now thought to have a quick and varied influence on fertility. This means that individuals, by responding to their social, economic and environmental circumstances by earlier or later marriage, could have a marked influence on demographic trends. Such a notion is supported by the fact that after 1500 the age of marriage among the lower orders in England (27-8 for men and 24-7 for women) was later than in the rest of Western Europe. This suggests that in England people were reacting to worsening economic conditions by having smaller families. Indeed, as the age of marriage among the lower orders tended to rise slightly during the seventeenth century when economic conditions were improving, it can be said that people were positively trying to better their economic position. In contrast, elite English men and women, following the general Western European pattern, tended to marry in their early twenties or sooner. However, this is more understandable because, unlike the continental lower orders, they enjoyed a high standard of living.

## a) The Family

The English family was nuclear and not extended. The average family size is calculated to have been 4.5, and typically to have consisted of parents, eldest son, very young children, and apprentices or servants. It was also normal practice among all social groups for the head of the household to provide for his widowed mother, if he had one. There were variations in this pattern which reflected social, cultural and economic differences. Aristocratic family groups were generally much larger. They often consisted of parents, married sons and daughters, younger children and children from other families who were being educated in the household, estate officials and large numbers of servants. This reflected the high social status, great wealth and considerable political and administrative responsibility of the aristocracy. Inheritance customs could have an effect on family formation. In England it was normal for the eldest son to inherit the family property which meant that the younger children of the lesser elites and the lower orders tended to leave home in their teens. Younger sons of the lesser elites generally went to school and then on to university and a legal training at the Inns of Court, while daughters were married off to suitable husbands. Among the lower orders younger children of both sexes left home in their early teens to become apprentices or servants in husbandry or industry. However, in parts of Kent and some other woodland and forest areas the custom was for partible inheritance, under which all children were entitled to share in the property. Families were larger in these areas because both married and unmarried children were more likely to stay at home. The expansion of rural industry in open forest, woodland and fenlands also influenced family size in those areas. Children were less likely to leave home until they married because there was plenty of employment available and all the family could contribute to the household economy.

## b) Fertility

Fertility was largely dependent upon the role of women within or outside the family. In a patriarchal society women were expected to bear children and raise a family, and to be subservient to their husbands. Additionally, lower-order wives had to contribute their share to the family economy by work inside or outside the home. Single women (discounting female apprentices and servants who were part of their master's family) were regarded with distrust, and given abusive titles, such as 'whore', 'spinster' or 'old maid'. Similarly, barren women or those guilty of infidelity were seen as outcasts. That it was not considered possible for men to be infertile, and that male adultery was thought acceptable, shows the apparently (see page 100) wide support within society for such female stereotyping. The stress on female fertility and faithfulness within marriage among the elites is understandable. For them it was essential to produce a legitimate male heir to preserve the family name and estates. The failure of elite women to bear male children was a cause of the demise of many aristocratic and gentry families. The importance of children (whether legitimate or illegitimate) to lower-order families is less clear. Most children left home and rarely returned except for visits, and there was no social obligation on them to support old and infirm parents.

Rates of illegitimacy did have some effect on total fertility. At the same time they help to explain social attitudes and the workings of the social, economic and demographic system. Illegitimate births, despite women's reputation for having insatiable and unrestrained sexual desires, were comparatively few in number. However, they were closely linked with pre-nuptial pregnancy and to some extent with economic conditions. During the second half of the sixteenth century illegitimate births rose to 3.4 per cent, then fell to 0.9 per cent by the 1650s, only to rise again to 3.1 per cent by the early eighteenth century. Over the same period pre-nuptial pregnancies (calculated on first births taking place within eight months of marriage) followed a roughly similar pattern. About 31 per cent of pregnancies up to 1600 are thought to have been pre-nuptial. This figure fell to 16 per cent by the end of seventeenth century, but rose to 22 per cent in the early eighteenth century. It is thought that many illegitimate births were the result of pre-marital sex between couples who were then prevented from marrying through worsening economic circumstances.

But, although this theory would explain the late sixteenth-century increase, it would not account for the rise after 1650 when economic conditions were improving. Possibly the increasing geographical mobility and the weakening of village communities may have had some influence. Among the elites illegitimate births were often concealed, and bastards were generally provided for by the father or relatives. However, pregnant servants were frequently thrown out of the family and had to be supported by the parish. This illustrates the double standard that existed between elites and the rest of society. Illegitimacy among the lower orders carried a considerable social stigma, especially for the woman who was generally presumed to have been the guilty party. Pregnant girls with no prospective husband were sent to houses of correction, or just driven out of the parish to prevent them and their children being a charge on the parish rate. Many such girls went into towns and took up prostitution as the only means by which they could earn a living.

## c) Single Women

It has been calculated that about one in eight women did not marry and this is thought to have had a significant impact on general levels of fertility. Such a figure is arrived at by taking a cohort of women born in particularly well recorded parishes and tracing them to see which ones did not marry or have children over a 45-year period. On this basis it is thought that 5 per cent of women remained unmarried in the late sixteenth century, and that this figure rose to 22 per cent during the seventeenth century. Such an increase may well offer an explanation why the population level was falling or stagnating in the late seventeenth century. A decision not to marry seems to have been related to economic conditions, but not in the same way as marriage age because more women appear not have married when the economy was actually improving. The reason for this may have been that in times of economic depression women were forced to marry for survival, whereas more chose to stay single when employment prospects were better. However, as the figure for female celibacy had fallen back to 12 per cent by the early eighteenth century when employment was even more buoyant, there may well have been other reasons. Another explanation for this trend may be that increased migration created sexual imbalances. In some towns there was a surplus of young women which meant that many of them were denied the opportunity to marry. Similarly, the movement of young men to the colonies or to open parishes and towns probably limited the chance of marriage for those girls left behind.

## d) The Influence of Fertility on the Demographic Pattern

As most women did marry, nuptial age was probably the most volatile influence on population levels. Younger marriage by women not only increased the number of children being born, but also, by reducing the time-span between generations, further expanded total fertility. During the seventeenth century the average marriage age for lower-order men remained constant at 28.1, while that for women rose from 25.6 to 26.2. Then in the early eighteenth century the marriage age for both sexes fell; for men to 27.2 and for women to 25.4. This move towards later marriage in the seventeenth century is considered to have been the result of the adverse economic conditions of the late sixteenth century. It used to be thought that, as far as age of marriage was concerned, reaction to poor economic situations was slow and moved in waves covering about 40 years. It is now thought that society responded more quickly, taking only 15 to 20 years to adjust. This means that the later age of marriage in the seventeenth century is seen as being a positive move towards improving standards of living rather than as being merely a delayed reaction to adversity. The increase in marriage age among women would certainly have reduced total fertility. Furthermore, during the seventeenth century between 25 and 30 per cent of all marriages were re-marriages caused by the death of one of the partners. Although most people re-married after about a year the effect was probably to reduce total fertility still further because it appears that there was a greater gap between children produced in second and subsequent marriages than in first marriages.

## e) Marriage

Marriage was based on economic circumstances, opportunity, and, for the lower orders, personal choice. The age of consent in England was 14 for boys and 12 for girls, except between 1653 and 1660 when the ages were raised to 16 and 14 respectively. However, among lower-order girls only one in eight is recorded as marrying in her teens, while only two out of five aristocratic girls were not married by the age of 20. For most of the lower orders getting married in church had to fit into the pattern of the agricultural seasons. This meant that in pastoral areas most marriages occurred during April and May, while in arable parishes the peak months were September and October. Conception generally took place after harvesting, so that most baptisms are recorded in January, February and March. Burials, because many of them were the result of winter epidemics, cold and food shortages, also tended to peak in the same months. In the towns and areas of rural industry births, burials and marriages were spread evenly throughout the year. However, as marriage in church was not a legal requirement until 1753, many marriages, burials and births may have gone unrecorded. An exchange of vows before witnesses, or consent followed by sexual intercourse were both regarded as legal forms of marriage by the Church. It is estimated that at least 18 per cent of all seventeenth-century marriages did not take place in church, and this may well be an underestimate. Marriage age was lower in open parishes, and more people were likely to marry outside the Church because ecclesiastical control tended to be weaker in these areas. Moreover, marriage, baptismal and 'churching' (the ritual cleansing of women after childbirth before they could re-enter church) customs varied widely between parishes. This makes it difficult to fully assess the extent and importance of marriage among the lower orders.

## f) Fertility or Mortality as a Determinant of Population Change.

At present, levels of mortality and fertility are seen as being equally important, and to have acted as a balance to each other. Between 1571 and 1611 fertility and mortality are considered to have been stable, while from 1611 to 1671 fertility fell and mortality increased. Low fertility is thought to have been the main cause of population stagnation in the late seventeenth century, while mortality slowed down any demographic expansion in the early eighteenth century. It was once thought that unhygienic conditions and poor midwifery caused a high incidence of death in childbirth which may have had some influence on the balance between fertility and mortality. However, it is now calculated that woman ran at the most only a 7 per cent risk of dying in childbirth, which was no higher than mortality among both sexes from disease, accidents and other causes. One thing that is clear is that fertility was considerably higher among the elites than the lower orders. Apart from a lower marriage age, elite women generally had their babies put out to wet nurses, while lower-order women breast fed their infants. Breast feeding increased the interval between births and so lowered fertility, but, milk from the natural mother supposedly being more nutritious, may well have reduced infant mortality. Whether or not the practice among elite women of not breast feeding their children increased the risk of infant mortality is undecided.

## 5 Migration and Changes in Population Distribution

The influence of migration on the demographic pattern of Stuart England was highly significant. Not only did it cause variations in the levels of fertility and mortality, but it changed the overall distribution of population. Until the seventeenth century most people had lived in the countryside, and the main concentration of population had been in the south-east of England. By the eighteenth century a noticeable shift of population to the Midlands and the north of England had already taken place and there had been a marked increase in the size and number of towns. This shift in population was largely the result of young people moving out of the closed fielden parishes of the South where employment prospects were limited. They went either to expanding older towns, or to the open parishes of the Midlands and North where land and employment in rural industry were available. The expansion of London and many older towns, where mortality rates were high, was mainly because of the sheer number of migrants. Growth in the open parishes equally resulted from the increasing volume of migrants, but, also, in many cases from higher fertility rates. The consequence for some fielden parishes and decaying older towns was depopulation.

### a) Migration and Re-Settlement

The government and local authorities were well aware of this trend. Like the Tudors they regarded this type of movement as causing social instability and were anxious to prevent it. At the same time migration was officially linked with poverty and vagrancy and was seen as undermining the provisions of the poor laws. For these reasons a variety of legislation was passed to limit the free movement and re-settlement of people around the country. These measures culminated with the Settlement Law of 1662. This was intended to revise and reinforce the existing legislation against vagrancy.

Care was to be taken that the poor had certificates of settlement in the parish where they lived. Churchwardens and overseers of the poor was ordered to round up illegal migrants and present them before the local justices of the peace so that they could be sent back to their parishes of origin. The only exception was to be seasonal harvest workers who were to be allowed to move freely as long as they had a certificate of settlement. Needless to say the Act was just as difficult to enforce as its predecessors. It did possibly curtail some longer distance subsistence migration, although the reduction in this type of migration might just have been the result of improved employment opportunities and the halt in population increase.

Increasing migration, whether internally or overseas, was the result both of improved transport and communications and of changing economic opportunities. A large proportion of such movement was only over a short distance - up to ten miles. This was mainly subsistence migration with families and servants in husbandry moving home or taking up new employment in a neighbouring parish without expecting greatly to improve their economic circumstances. Betterment migration was generally over a relatively longer distance. Children of the wealthier sections of society travelled to take up apprenticeships, to be educated at university and the Inns of Court, or to seek employment in elite households, the professions and commerce. Long-distance internal migration of some hundred miles or more was generally limited to the wealthy and vagrants. Landowners and merchants travelled for pleasure, and for social, political and business reasons. Many young vagrants of both sexes moved to settle and make a fresh start to life in a different part of the country. The most distant form of re-settlement was emigration to the colonies in the New World or to Ireland. Although the rate of emigration was slowing down during the seventeenth century, an estimated net total of 54,400 people left England to settle abroad. A large proportion of these, like the vagrants, were in the age range of 15 to 24 and one in four were women.

All these projections on migration are very hypothetical and the impact on population distribution is still not clear. Although it is uncertain how many emigrants eventually returned to England, their departure is thought to have been the reason for the slight fall in England's population in the second half of the century. Moreover, the removal of a significant section of the most fertile age group is considered to have slowed demographic recovery. As many of the emigrants seem to have been more skilled and literate than average they are classified as betterment migrants. They often left England even when economic conditions were improving because they judged that prospects were better in the colonies. The effect of internal migration is even more difficult to calculate. Short-distance and seasonal movement only had a localised influence on demographic distribution. Betterment migration by the children of the more affluent sections of society and long-distance travelling by the wealthy involved only a relatively small number of people and generally did not result in permanent settlement. It appears that the young vagrants moving to settle in old and new towns or the open parishes of the North and the Midlands were mainly responsible for the relocation of population. Like the young emigrants they were trying to improve their standard of living, and so this can be seen as migration for betterment rather than for subsistence, as it was at the end of the sixteenth century. By the late seventeenth century most people were travelling shorter distances as the economy expanded and permanent employment was easier to find. At the same time, there was an increase in seasonal migration in response to the growing specialisation in industry and agriculture. Much of this industrial growth was in the north of England which meant that the region was becoming even more attractive than the capital. In 1500, 51 per cent of London's apprentices had come from the northern counties, but by the early eighteenth century only 4 per cent were recruited from the North, while 72 per cent were drawn from the Home Counties.

## b) Demographic Growth in London and Other Towns

Even so the most striking demographic growth was in the towns, particularly London. It has been estimated that one person in six of the entire population lived in, worked in, or visited the capital at some period of their life. In 1600 London had a population of 190,000, which had reached 400,000 by 1650 and had risen to 575,000 by 1700. This rapid increase during the seventeenth century is calculated to have needed 900,000 migrants, which absorbed some 8 per cent of the natural increase for the whole of England. Such expansion was the consequence of London's position as a capital city, a national and international market, and a social, educational and cultural centre. Thereafter the continued growth in the Midlands and the North slowed the rate of expansion, and by 1750 the capital's population had grown to only 675,000. By way of comparison, Norwich, England's second largest town and a major industrial textile centre, had a population of only just under 30,000 by 1700. However, this represented a doubling of the town's inhabitants during the seventeenth century. A number of the other older towns also continued to expand. Bristol, a centre for Atlantic and slave trading and the new industries of tobacco manufacture and sugar refining, increased in numbers from 12,000 to 21,000 over the same period. Other older ports such as Newcastle upon Tyne, York, Yarmouth, Colchester and Exeter, benefited from the commercial expansion and had populations of over 10,000 by the end the century. Traditional industrial centres such as Nottingham, Coventry, Leicester, Worcester and Bury St Edmunds responded to renewed economic activity and had populations of between 5,000 and 10,000 by 1700. A very significant development was the growth of new towns. Liverpool, specialising along the same lines as Bristol, had a population of 700 in the mid-sixteenth century. By the 1700 this had increased to 7,000 and by 1750 had reached 22,000. A number of the new industrial centres were experiencing similar expansion. The population of Birmingham had risen to 10,000 by 1700, while Leeds, Bradford, Manchester and Sunderland all had more than 5,000 inhabitants by the same date. Although the vast majority of people still lived in the countryside these changes represent a significant move towards urbanisation. It is estimated that in 1600 255,000 people lived in towns with a population of 10,000 or more, which was 5.8 per cent of the population. By 1700 this figure had increased to 718,000 - 13.3 per cent of the population, of which of which 11.5 per cent lived in London.

## c) Areas of New and Industrial Settlement

The other major trend during the seventeenth century was for a movement of population away from the South East into the Midlands and North. This was the result of both migration and faster demographic growth in the industrialised open parishes. It has been calculated that population in the Cambridgeshire fens and the north-western counties grew at twice the rate of Norfolk and Suffolk. However, such increases were not consistent or even. Staffordshire and the fenlands expanded for most of the century, but in Cumbria population rose until 1600, then fell until the 1640s, and then started to expand again. Much of the demographic expansion resulted from the settlement of cottagers in areas such as the Forest of Dean in Gloucestershire and Rockingham Forest in Northamptonshire. In the majority of these areas industrial activity, especially textiles and metalworking, was becoming more important than agriculture. This led to the development of predominantly industrial parishes, like those around Sheffield, each of which specialised in producing a different type of metal tool. Gradually such parishes merged together to form industrial conurbations such as Wolverhampton and Dudley. It is thought that the expanding choice of employment which attracted migrants and allowed earlier marriage led to a population growth possibly 35 per cent faster than in fielden parishes. However, this theory has not yet been fully proved, and it has been suggested that employers moved into areas of existing high demographic growth because they offered a good supply of cheap labour.

## 6 Inflation and the Standard of Living

Although the course of inflation over the period is relatively clear it is much more difficult to determine its effect on standards of living. The reason for this is the great regional and local diversity and the variations in fortune between and within sections of society. The low marriage age among the elites suggests that their prospects in general were continuing to improve. However, later marriage among the lower orders cannot be assumed to show a continued fall in their expectations as it is thought that many people were trying to improve their living standards by having fewer children.

## a) Inflation

Prices are thought to have risen seven-fold between 1500 and 1650 and then to have stagnated with a slight rise of some 3 per cent by 1700. At the same time increased production meant that the price of industrial consumer goods rose at a slightly slower rate than the general price index and brought them into the price range of a larger section of society. However, attempts have recently been made to revise these statistics and it may be that the rate of inflation was actually slightly lower. Up to 1650 wages rose only three-fold which represented a 50 per cent reduction in real terms. By the early eighteenth century wages had increased by some 4 per cent, with industrial wages rising more than those for agriculture. The main reason for these changes was the sharp fall in the rate of population increase. This removed the pressure on resources, especially for foodstuffs. At the same time the pool of surplus labour was reduced which forced up wages. Another effect of the slow-down in demographic growth was to change the age structure of the population. This had considerable impact on the standard of living which is seen as being dependent upon the balance between the resources-producing and the wealth-consuming sections of society. Those people in the age group from 15 to 59 are seen as being self-supporting or producers of resources, while those above the age of 60 and below the age of 14 are classified as consuming wealth. While the proportion of the population over the age of 60 remained stable at between 7 and 10 per cent, that for the under 14-year-olds fell from about 37 per cent in the late sixteenth century to around 29 per cent by the 1670s. An additional deflationary influence is thought to have been an improvement in the money supply. More finance and banking facilities (see page 88) meant that there was an increase in bonds, cheques and paper money in circulation which helped to keep prices down by reducing pressure on the coinage.

## b) Living Standards: Landowners, Yeomen and Husbandmen

Although, in general, living standards improved after the 1660s, the effect varied widely. Static or falling food prices and higher wages meant that landowners and husbandmen were potentially worse off. It was no longer possible to rely just on rising prices and cheap labour to make a profit, and levels of production had to be increased. This entailed greater investment in the land to improve yields through enclosure and specialisation in new crops and techniques. While the greater landowners and the more substantial yeomen and husbandmen had the resources to be able to undertake such improvements, many of the smaller landowners and husband-men could not afford the additional outlay. This was especially true after 1660 because of the disruption caused by the Civil War. The result of this situation was that the aristocracy and greater gentry tended to consolidate and increase their share of the land. In addition, to improve efficiency and to maintain their income from rents, they created larger leasehold farms by amalgamating smaller customary and copyhold tenancies. This resulted in many of the poorer husbandmen being forced off the land, especially after the 1670s. At the same time, many of the lesser gentry and yeomen found improvement costs too great and were forced to sell their estates to greater landowners. It has been claimed that this effectively ended the rise of the gentry and the yeomen which had been in progress since the fifteenth century. Although there is still much debate on the topic, it is generally agreed that a new landowning pattern had been created which was dominated by the great estate and the large leasehold farm (see chapters 2 and 5).

## c) Middle-Order Living Standards

The growing prosperity among the non-landed elites and those engaged in the professions, administration, finance, commerce and industry can be linked less directly to demographic change and the rate of inflation. Urban expansion, which was an important element in middle-order affluence, was a result of demographic change, but, equally, it was a consequence and a cause of economic growth. The middling groups in society were benefiting from the greater opportunities of investment or employment created by the upturn in the economy. To a considerable extent this can be attributed to the slowing down in the rate of inflation which extended the spending power of the general public. This led to an increase in demand which in turn encouraged investment and so created a consumer society. The middle orders were anxious to emulate the lifestyle of the landed elites and used their increasing wealth to buy more luxury and consumer goods. This encouraged more investment and higher output, which reduced production costs and so brought down prices. These cheaper goods then fell into the price range of groups lower down in society, and so there was a further increase in demand. The so-called 'trickle down' effect promoting consumerism is considered to be highly important in creating England's commercial supremacy in the eighteenth century (see chapters 3, 4, and 5).

## d) The Lower-Order Standard of Living

The effect of the change in the demographic and inflationary pattern on the lower orders continues to be the subject of debate and controversy. A pessimistic view of the situation is that increased agricultural specialisation forced more smallholders off the land and created a countryside dominated by large commercial farms and growing numbers of landless labourers. Furthermore, although an improvement in real wages helped to alleviate abject poverty and starvation, the gap between rich and poor was growing even more rapidly. Moreover, because the successful middling groups were emulating the lifestyles of the elites there was an increasing cultural rift within society. This led to social, economic and cultural polarisation, with wealthy, educated patricians on one side, and the poor, illiterate and ungodly masses on the other. The more optimistic interpretation is that agricultural improvements had removed the spectre of subsistence crises, famine and starvation. At the same time, economic expansion was creating much greater employment, so that many more people were benefiting from the rise in real wages. Although, there was still widespread poverty, the poor laws were working efficiently and prevented any section being in dire distress. Indeed, it is suggested that there was increased spending power among the lower orders, and that this was beginning to create a mass market for consumer goods (see chapters 3, 6 and 7).

---

***Making notes on*** *'Population, Urban Change and the Standard of Living'*

Even though many historians no longer regard the mid-seventeenth century as an economic and social watershed, there is little doubt that the 1650s mark a significant demographic change. Falling or stagnating population levels are thought to have brought improved employment and living standards for a large proportion of the masses. However, historical demography is based on fragmentary evidence which is difficult to interpret and its analysis is often controversial. The first section examines the sources used to calculate population change, fertility, mortality and migration. You should note how the evidence is used, and what are the difficulties in making an accurate back projection of early modern population patterns. The second section discusses the differing interpretations of population change. It is important to pay particular attention to why it is thought that England, unlike the rest of Western Europe, had escaped from the problem of recurrent subsistence crises. Section 3 considers the levels of disease and mortality during the period and the debate over whether mortality or fertility had the major impact on population levels. Careful consideration needs to be given to the effects of migration, increased geographical mobility and urban growth before deciding on the importance of mortality on restricted population growth. The fourth section assesses the various arguments in favour of fertility being the major determinant of demographic movement. You should consider very carefully before deciding if late marriage was part of a balanced social, economic and demographic system that enabled England to escape from subsistence crises. Section 5 looks at the various ways in which migration was altering the distribution of population in England. A careful assessment needs to be made of the causes and consequences of urban growth and the development of new areas of rural industry in the Midlands and North West. The final section examines changes in the cost of living and the extent to which this was influenced by variations in population levels and distribution. Particular attention needs to be paid to how and why living standards changed both between and within different sections of society.

---

*Answering essay questions on* 'Population, Urban Change and the Standard of Living'

All three of the topics discussed in this chapter are highly controversial and as such are likely to be selected for attention by examiners. Past experience suggests that 'population' is likely to appear on examination papers much more frequently than 'urban change' and 'standard of living'. However, as the topics are interconnected and might be linked together for consideration, it would be unwise to prepare yourself to answer questions on any of them in isolation. The following questions suggest that this is so.

1   How far was the general improvement in living standards in England after 1650 due to a slow-down in the increase of population?
2   'The increase in England's population during the seventeenth century was primarily due to a decline in the death rate.' Do you agree?
3   To what extent is it valid to talk of an 'urban renaissance' in Stuart England?
4   What were the results of England's rise in population during the seventeenth century?
5   Why did English towns (other than London) experience a modest increase in the size of their populations between 1600 and 1700?

Many candidates in examinations automatically assume that 'What?' and 'Why?' questions (such as questions 4 and 5 above) are easier to answer than 'challenging statement' and 'How far/to what extent?' questions (such as questions 1, 2 and 3 above). This is often, but by no means always, a safe assumption. If you try to assess the level of

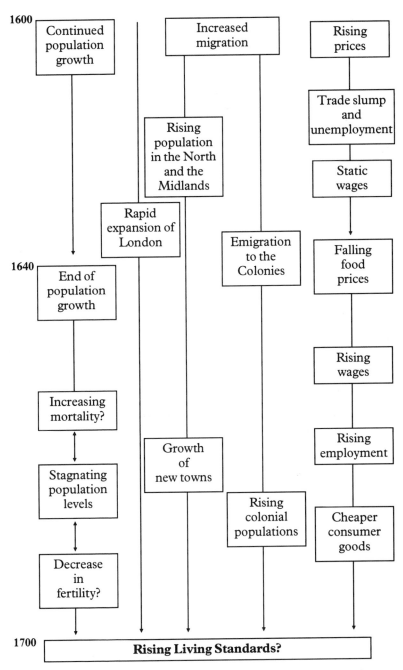

*Summary - Population, Urban Change and the Standard of Living*

difficulty of each of the five questions above you may come to the conclusion that questions 4 and 5 are as difficult as any of the others. You should have found that in order to make your assessment you needed to examine the wording of each question carefully. In question 4 there is a phrase that would need to be 'unpacked' in some detail in the introductory paragraph of the answer. What is it? What makes the question quite complicated is the need to discuss the differing views of historians. How would this need to be reflected in the plan for your answer? Question 5 will need to be answered by more than a number of 'because' points. The question contains a very large assumption that will require a full discussion. What is this assumption? You may now feel that questions 1, 2 and 3 are relatively straightforward!

***Source-based questions on** 'Population, Urban Change and the Standard of Living'*

**1 Government Attempts to Reduce Unemployment, 1621-2**
Carefully read the extract from the letter sent by the Privy Council to JPs in clothmaking counties, given on page 24. Answer the following questions.
a)  Explain the two things that JPs are being ordered to do. (6 marks)
b)  What, is it claimed, has the government done to improve the situation for clothiers? (2 marks)
c)  Based on evidence from the extract, describe and comment on the government's motives for wishing to reduce unemployment among textile workers. (6 marks)
d)  To what extent was the letter likely to have had its desired effect? Explain your answer. (6 marks)

# CHAPTER 3

# The Economy: The Agricultural and Industrial Sectors

## 1 Introduction: Issues and Approaches

Until comparatively recently the Stuart economy has not been considered particularly dynamic. It tended to be regarded as an uninteresting period sandwiched between the spectacular population growth and inflation under the Tudors and the glamour of the beginnings of industrial growth in the eighteenth century. England was thought to have shared the crises, stagnation and depression experienced by most of Western Europe. Interest centred mainly on the great debate over the English Civil War and speculation over the commercial impact of the 'bourgeois revolution'.

The 'watershed' of the Civil War was regarded as having ushered in a new spirit of progressive, economic individualism. This, it was considered, was the driving force of the English commercial and agricultural revolutions which in turn led to the first Industrial Revolution. It was this preoccupation with the origins of the industrialisation that dictated a great deal of the analysis of the early modern economy. Four main areas, population, agriculture, commerce and industry, were identified as being essential to create the economic growth which eventually culminated in the Industrial Revolution. However, there was no agreement about which of these sectors was the most significant, or about how they interacted with each other. Consequently a variety of general theories were put forward to explain why the English economy and society was essentially different from those of its continental neighbours. This, it was thought, would provide the answer to the question why England was the first country to industrialise. Most of these theories assumed that a revolutionary change took place within English society which allowed it to diverge from the still essentially peasant communities in the rest of Europe. This approach is now out of favour with a majority of economic historians. Much greater emphasis is put on continuity, and the notion of slow evolutionary progress has replaced that of sudden revolutionary leaps forward.

### a) The General State of the Economy

This change of approach has meant that the Stuart economy is again being studied in its own right rather than just as a staging post in the process towards industrialisation. Undoubtedly there was a great deal of continuity from the sixteenth century. What needs to be decided is whether any distinctive changes were taking place and, if there were, in which sectors they were occurring. Seventeenth-century England was still an overwhelmingly rural society and most economic activity was based on agriculture. In economic terms the century can be divided into two halves. During the first 50 years conditions appeared to be very similar to those of the late sixteenth century. Population levels continued to rise, inflation was high, wages were low and unemployment was high. In contrast, after the 1650s, there was demographic stagnation, inflation was low, wages rose and employment opportunities expanded. To explain such a marked dissimilarity it is necessary to decide whether this was the result of steady development within the existing economy or whether there had been a sequence of dramatic changes.

## b) Indicators of Economic Change

Economists consider that a number of indicators can be used as evidence of economic progress. Within an essentially agricultural society the paramount sign of more advanced economic activity is thought to be a change in employment patterns. This is shown by an increasing number of people moving from what are considered to be low-level economic occupations, such as farm labouring, forestry and fishing, to take up more skilled work in manufacturing, service industries and the professions. Such a development requires greater agricultural specialisation and production to allow labour to move to towns and industrial areas and still be fed. For this to be achieved there has to be a high level of investment in both agriculture and industry, which means that an ample supply of money and an efficient financial sector are necessary. At the same time there has to be an increase in demand which might result from population growth or an improvement in living standards. To meet increased demand there has to be efficient marketing of both domestic and overseas foodstuffs and manufactured goods. This, in turn, means that there has to be an effective communications system by land and sea for the distribution of goods and services.

## c) The Problems of the Sources used for Statistics

At first sight it seems that it should be quite easy to apply these economic indicators to the Stuart economy. Today, with sophisticated computers, elaborate census material, trade and production statistics, and inflation and unemployment figures, economic analysts can almost instantly detect any changes in the economy. However, the almost complete absence of any reliable data for early modern England makes it difficult for the historian to discern more than the broadest economic trends. For example, the fragmentary and unreliable nature of parish registers and other demographic sources means that calculations of population levels and movement are at the best very speculative (see page 16).

For similar reasons it is equally difficult to gain any clear picture of occupational structures, particularly as any individual could have several jobs. Variations in wages between different occupations and between regions of the country add to the problems of determining living standards. This situation is further complicated by the fact that in many cases family income depended on the earnings of two adults, and possibly of several children. In any case, the movement of prices and calculations of inflation rates are largely based on the Phelps Brown and Hopkins index of prices which applies only to the south of England. Commercial statistics are equally fragmentary and potentially misleading. There are few reliable overseas trade figures before the eighteenth century, and those that do exist are mostly for goods entering and leaving London. To add to the confusion, there was no national uniformity of weights, measures, lengths and sizes. Furthermore, goods might keep the same name, but change in size, quality and composition over time, and so the historian is never fully confident that like is being compared with like. Most importantly, significantly more than half of national production and trade was generated in the domestic market, and the overwhelming majority of this went entirely unrecorded.

## 2 Problems of the Late Tudor and Early Stuart Economy

Until the 1640s the English economy remained in a very depressed condition. This situation was caused by basic weaknesses in the late Tudor economy which showed no signs of being resolved until the middle of the seventeenth century.

### a) Lack of Demand and Growth in the Tudor Economy

The Elizabethan economy had most of the theoretical requirements for economic growth in place. However, by 1600 the English economy was still small scale and relatively unadvanced. Although the population had doubled to about four million during the sixteenth century, it was only two-thirds of the level reached before the Black Death in 1349 (see page 7). Moreover, although there had been considerable urban migration from the countryside, the proportion of the population living in towns was still below 6 per cent. London was the only large town. It had increased in population from about 60,000 to just under 200,000 during the century. Most other towns had tended to stagnate. For example, the population of Norwich, the next largest city after London, had only risen from 12,000 in 1500 to 15,000 in 1600. This meant that the vast majority of the population still lived in small and relatively isolated rural communities. Consequently most demographic expansion had taken place in the countryside and had little impact on demand. Often towns were too small to create a market demand beyond their immediate vicinity. Even the expansion of London was not large enough to have much impact outside the Home Counties. In any case, road, river and coastal communications, although being improved, were not good enough yet to form a national network linking London with the provinces. For this reason, the rising demand for grain in the capital had to be met largely by corn imported from the Baltic. Hence, although the population expansion did encourage some commercial farming and specialisation, it was located only in the vicinity of the larger and expanding towns.

Another aspect of the limited amount of growth and demand created by the population increase within the Tudor economy was the distribution of wealth. Demographic expansion had been accompanied by rapid inflation which amounted to about 400 per cent over the sixteenth century as a whole. For the great mass of the people this meant that their living standards had been eroded by rising food prices, increasing rents and static wages. The only sections of society to benefit from the inflationary situation were the landed elites and, to a lesser extent, those engaged in commerce and industry. As they represented less than 10 per cent of the population, their increased spending power did not have a great effect on overall demand within the economy. They had very little incentive to invest money in improving their land or business concerns because steadily rising prices and rents ensured increasing profits without the risk of capital outlay. Instead, the elites spent their money on house-building, improving their lifestyle and buying luxury goods. As most of these were not produced in England, the great majority of the luxury items had to be imported from abroad. The result of this was to worsen the trade balance without giving any stimulus to the economy.

## b) Agricultural Problems

It was this lack of demand and incentive to invest that kept the Tudor economy small and curtailed economic growth. The agricultural sector showed a few signs of commercialisation and greater specialisation, but no real expansion had materialised by 1600. Most landowners were content to profit from increased prices and rents without undertaking agricultural improvements. Similarly, as yeomen and husbandmen could generally afford to pay the higher rents for their farms out of the higher prices they received for the crops and livestock they sold, they too did not change their methods. Consequently, the enclosure of land for specialist farming, the growing of a wider range of crops and the adoption of new techniques took place only spasmodically. Moreover, much of the enclosure that did take place in the sixteenth century was for sheep runs - because the high price of wool brought a good return on the investment until the 1580s - rather than to allow improvements in arable heritage ignored?

farming. In any case, successive Tudor governments, although encouraging arable farming, legislated against enclosure because they feared that it caused depopulation and threatened social stability.

Generally the size of farming operations remained small scale. Some rising gentry and yeomen (see page 8) established larger commercial operations, but most farms were held by husbandmen with under 60 acres, and were labour intensive with low per capita yields. At the same time, a number of subsistence smallholders were being forced to leave the land because they could not afford the rising rents - they had little surplus production to sell at enhanced prices. Even more significantly many younger sons were unable to marry and take over smallholdings because of the competition for land caused by rising population. Although regional specialisation (see page 52) was beginning in some areas, because of the poor communication system and the absence of a national market, most foodstuffs were grown to meet local requirements. This created another problem in that as most people lived in the countryside and had some access to land there was still considerable self-sufficiency which meant that demand was very sluggish, especially in good harvest years. It was only after the 1580s, when wool prices began to fall because demand for English cloth on the continent was declining, that more attention was paid to growing grain. In consequence, England was producing barely enough cereals to feed the growing population. It is true that the country managed to avoid recurrent subsistence crises. However, some grain always had to be imported to feed London. Such imports increased at times of harvest failure, especially during runs of bad harvests, such as the mid-1590s.

## c) Industrial Problems

Industry was faced with similar problems. The only major manufactured export was unfinished cloth, produced by the rural cottage industry, which was sent to the Netherlands for finishing and distribution. The industry was organised by capitalistic 'clothiers', who supervised the stages of manufacture and controlled the marketing. Although there was a division of labour, manufacture was labour intensive, being carried out in the home using hand tools. Apart from the manufacture of woollen cloth, English industry was small scale, craft based and with little division of labour. The most specialised and best quality goods, including dyed and finished cloth, were manufactured in the towns, especially London, under guild control. Craft guilds were organisations of master craftsmen, and only those who had served a seven-year apprenticeship could become members. They produced small quantities of expensive goods for sale locally. Similar, cheaper and generally poorer quality craft manufactures were made in the countryside, but by a less skilled labour force which often had not served an apprenticeship. During the sixteenth century urban and rural industries were in opposition to each other. The guilds complained that the rural industries used unskilled labour and produced shoddy goods which competed unfairly with their own better finished products. The government generally supported the guilds and passed legislation, such as the Statute of Artificers of 1563, which tried to limit manufacturing to the towns and to ensure that all industrial workers served apprenticeships. However, this legislation was generally ignored, so it did not halt the spread of industry in the countryside.

Limited industrial expansion and investment meant that many of the smallholders being forced off the land by commercialisation could not find industrial work. This was a problem made worse by the additional labour force being created by population increase. It was this situation that caused widespread poverty and vagrancy during the second half of the sixteenth century. The Statute of Artificers was one of a series of measures taken by Elizabethan governments to try to overcome these problems. The major fear of the authorities was that too many people leaving the land would undermine agriculture, cause depopulation and lead to social instability. A number of vagrancy and poverty measures were passed which culminated in the 1601 Poor Law Act. This established a system which provided for the relief and some work for the impotent poor in rural parishes and maintained workhouses in the towns. However, as the intention was to prevent the poor unemployed from moving around freely, the legislation hampered the unemployed from finding work. At the same time the Elizabethan governments were trying to raise the level of employment by establishing new industries. Patents were given to craftsmen, especially from the continent, willing to establish new industries or new techniques, such as glass making, paper making, pin making, or linen weaving. These patents gave the holders a monopoly of the new process for 20 years as long as they trained and employed an English labour force. Apart from trying to improve employment this policy aimed to improve the quality and to widen the range of English industrial goods so that fewer manufactures would have to be imported. Even though a considerable range of new ventures were set up, they had little impact on English industry by 1600. Unemployment levels were still high and large quantities of continental goods, ranging from tennis balls, looking glasses, combs and needles to soap, saws, vinegar, woad and yarn still had to be imported.

## d) The Lack of Overseas Trade

Although progress had been made towards establishing a broader industrial base, the failure of industry to expand and diversify had created considerable problems for the English economy by 1600. The Tudor economy had been essentially export-led, relying on the high demand for unfinished English cloth exports to the Netherlands. Because of the seemingly constant demand it was easy for English merchants to deal just with the Antwerp cloth buyers without bothering to find additional products to sell or alternative markets with which to trade. At the same time the elite demand for high quality manufactured goods not produced in England resulted in a lesser, but still significant, inflow of imports. Consequently, when the demand for English cloth dried up in the 1580s there was an urgent need to find new markets and alternative goods for export to offset the imbalance in trade. By the 1590s England was facing a serious trade recession, high unemployment, continuing population expansion and rising inflation. This situation was made even worse by harvest failures and widespread dearth and poverty.

## e) Causes of Change after the 1640s

The English economy remained depressed until the 1640s and then began to improve rapidly. This change of fortune has no one simple explanation because the seventeenth-century economy was basically similar to that of the previous century. However, one underlying cause of the change was that improvements to both agriculture and industry initiated by the Tudors came to fruition under the later Stuarts. Other circumstances favoured the economic recovery. The end of the demographic expansion and rapid inflation brought improved employment and better living standards for the great mass of the people. The same trend ended the easy profits for landowners, farmers and industrialists, and forced them into greater investment and commercialisation to maintain the level of their incomes. Another highly significant feature was the doubling of the population of London during the century. This is seen as having a considerable impact on the economy by creating a huge centre of demand, which by 1700 had become a national and world market. The resultant increase in demand meant that the seventeenth-century English economy had become import rather than export led because of the growing quantities of raw materials coming from the colonies and the Far East.

## 3 Developments in Agriculture

It is now widely agreed that there was no revolutionary change in English agriculture during the seventeenth and early eighteenth centuries. This is not to say that there were not some very significant developments based on the foundations established under the Tudors. A number of reasons have been advanced to explain why the agricultural sector had become so much more efficient by the end of the seventeenth century. The growth of London and its food markets clearly had a considerable impact on the nature and volume of demand. This in turn helped to promote regional specialisation and commercialisation, which was linked to the establishment of a national market. Specialist agriculture was itself dependent on improved communications as regions had to rely upon other areas to supply the foodstuffs that they no longer produced. Such commercialisation required a greater level of investment than had been present in the sixteenth century, when profit margins were maintained by rising prices. After the 1650s, when population levels stagnated, landowners and farmers had to become more efficient to survive. Consequently, they had to experiment with new techniques, crops and methods most suited to the soils they farmed. Many turned to growing industrial crops that offered good returns. This was linked with demand from domestic industry and the continuation of government policy of reducing the extent to which raw materials were imported by encouraging their production in England. During the seventeenth century increased agricultural efficiency was matched by the expansion of domestic industry, thereby allowing the transfer of labour between the two sectors.

## a) The Spread of Improved Methods and Techniques

Although there was a considerable increase in the geographical distribution of innovative crops and methods none of them were actually new. All the techniques practised by Stuart farmers had been introduced into England by the late sixteenth century. The great difference was that they were now used by large numbers of farmers all over the country, whereas previously many of the experiments had been limited to pioneering individuals. Part of the cause of this diffusion of ideas may have been increased levels of literacy (see page 99). Certainly it appears that by the 1640s a much higher proportion of gentry, yeomen and even husbandmen could read and write than was the case a hundred years before. Very few gentry and even fewer husbandmen would have been able to read John Fitzherbert's *Book of Husbandry* in 1523, or Sir Thomas Smith's *The Commonwealth of the Realm of England* in 1583. Many more would have studied books such as Sir Richard Weston's *Discourse on Husbandrie used in Brabant and Flanders* in 1645, or John Worlidge's *Systema Agriculturae* in 1669. It is equally significant that even by the turn of the century many gentry and yeomen, such as Robert Loader and John Blagrove from Berkshire, or Henry Best in Yorkshire were keeping detailed account books and diaries. But it must be remembered that although this development showed a rise in literacy, commercial rationality and a growing confidence in man's mastery of nature, it was still tinged by a belief in divine providence. This can be seen from Robert Loader's rueful comment in 1616 that 'This year in sowing too early I lost (the Lord being the cause thereof, but that the instrument wherewith it pleased him to work) ... the sum of £10 at least, so exceeding full was my barley with charlock [wild mustard]'. Another reason for the spread of agricultural improvement may well have been the increase in enclosure. It is estimated that in 1600 about 47 per cent of agricultural land was enclosed and that by 1700 the total had risen to 71 per cent, although much of this increase had occurred before 1650. Certainly after the 1650s governmental attitudes towards enclosure changed.

---

## Speeches in the House of Commons on Enclosures, 1601

1 Mr. Secretary Cecil said, I do not dwell in the country, I am not acquainted with the plough. But I think that whosoever doth not maintain the plough destroys this kingdom ... My motion therefore shall be that this law [for tillage and against enclosure] may not be
5 repealed, except former laws may be in force and revived. Say that a glut of corn should be, have we not sufficient remedy by transportation ... you shall never find [in any country] but that the ploughman is chiefly provided for, the neglect whereof will not only bring a general, but a particular damage to every man ... If we
10 bar tillage, we give scope to the depopulator; and then if the poor being thrust out of their houses go to dwell with others, straight we catch them with the Statute of Inmates; and if they wander abroad [move out of their own village] they are within danger of the Statute of the Poor to be whipped.

## Advice to the Stewards of Estates, 1731

1 A Steward should not forget to make the best enquiry into the disposition of any of the freeholders within or near any of his Lord's manors to sell their lands, that he may use his best endeavours to purchase them at as reasonable a price, as may be for
5 his Lord's advantage and convenience - especially in such manors, where improvements are to be made by inclosing commons and common-field; which (as every one, who is acquainted with the late improvement in agriculture, must know) is not a little advantageous to the nation in general, as well as highly profitable
10 to the undertaker [thereof] ... Whereas it is found, by long experience. that common or open fields, wherever they are suffered or continued, are great hindrances to a public good, and the honest improvement which every one might make of his own ... and, whereas the common objections hitherto raised against
15 inclosures are founded on mistakes, as if inclosures contributed either to hurt or ruin the poor; whilst it is plain that (when an inclosure is once resolved on) the poor will be employed for many years, in planting and preserving the hedges, and afterwards will be set to work both in the tillage and pasture, wherein they may get an
20 honest livelihood.

Previously the authorities had looked upon enclosure as a cause of depopulation and a threat to the stability of the social structure, and had rigorously legislated against the practice. After the 1650s the government saw enclosure as a means of economic improvement and a source of employment, and parliament began to pass private acts in order to encourage and speed up the process. Even so, it cannot be said that enclosure was absolutely necessary to introduce new crops and techniques successfully. For example, Oxfordshire, which remained largely unenclosed, was a leading area of agricultural improvement.

Whatever the cause, agricultural specialisation and improvement spread quite quickly in the seventeenth century. Improved techniques, such as floating water meadows to enhance grazing, along with better drainage and the use of artificial grasses like lucerne, sainfoin and clover, all helped to improve the balance between arable and pasture farming. Convertible husbandry to allow better rotation of crops, was being adopted widely. Crop rotation was improved by the use of root crops like potatoes, carrots and turnips - the latter, especially, being developed by the Walpole and Townshend families on their Norfolk estates. Marshlands in the Somerset Levels and the East Anglian fenlands were being drained and were found to be particularly suitable for industrial crops like woad and flax (see page 51). Experiments were carried out in various places to improve the composition of the soil by adding marl, lime or sand. Gradual improvements were made to farm machinery and equipment, such as ploughs, harrows and carts. The best known example was the seed drill patented by Jethro Tull in 1701. At the same time, because of the improved balance between arable and animal farming, there was more manure available to spread on the fields. This helped to increase yields, which were further enhanced by careful seed selection and the importation of improved seed stock from the Netherlands. Similarly, selective breeding of stock improved the size and quality of farm animals, particularly for meat production. All these processes were helped by the steady influx of Protestant refugees from the Netherlands, which was still the most advanced agricultural country in Europe. These immigrants, who settled mainly in the South East and East Anglia, were welcomed by the government for their industrial expertise (see page 57), but many of them introduced new agricultural and horticultural enterprises. Around London there was a great increase in vegetable growing, fruit orchards and market gardening. The cultivation and sale of flowers became an expanding business, especially around Norwich.

Alongside developments in food production, an increasing interest was shown in growing industrial crops. In part, this reflected a continued government policy of trying where possible to make England self-sufficient in raw materials in order to reduce imports. At the same time, the expansion and spread of domestic industry meant that such crops were profitable because of the rising demand (see page 58). The great majority of such crops had already been introduced into England during the sixteenth century. However, the trade depression from the 1590s to the 1620s, and the failure of the Cockayne Scheme of 1615 to improve the dyeing of woollen cloth, had dampened demand. Thereafter the growth of the textile and finishing trade all over the country encouraged their adoption by large- and small-scale growers alike. Flax and hemp were being grown widely to supply the linen and canvas trades. Linen thread was also in demand for use in the 'new draperies', in which it was mixed with wool, cotton or silk. Oil seed rape, linseed, hemp seed, woad, saffron, madder and weld were all grown to produce the oil and dyes needed by the textile trades. Oil seed rape grew particularly well on the drained fenland soils. A result of this was that the Cambridgeshire inland port of Wisbech became a major oil centre. By the early eighteenth century the town had seven oil crushing mills and was producing a thousand tons of oil a year. Woad was seen as a particularly useful crop by the government because it provided high levels of employment. It was grown widely in 50-acre plots in Oxfordshire and Gloucestershire, and it has been estimated that one acre of woad provided employment for four women and children for one-third of the year at a wage of fourpence a day. Barley was another crop which became very widely grown to supply the expanding brewing, distilling and vinegar industries. The technique for producing beer using hops, which unlike home-brewed ale would keep, had been introduced from the Netherlands. London became a major centre for brewing, and this encouraged the spread of hop growing in Kent and the Home Counties. Apart from their importance in supplying industry, industrial crops had a significant impact on demand within the economy. As their cultivation was generally labour intensive, they absorbed surplus labour and so gave many of the lower orders more money to spend. Similarly, as cash crops they gave the producers a higher return than they would have got from foodstuffs, and increased their spending power.

## b) The Diffusion of New Techniques and Specialisation

The spread and development of these crops and techniques gradually increased during the seventeenth century. The pace at which they occurred was very largely dependent on demand. Areas close to expanding towns, and in particular London, were likely to progress more rapidly than more isolated rural communities. Contrary to many previously-held beliefs, innovation was not dependent on the size of estates and farms. Many quite modest husbandmen appear to have been very ready to change their methods to meet new sources of demand. In any case, some forms of agriculture were more suitable to the small farm.

Tobacco was first grown in Winchcombe in Gloucestershire in 1619, but was banned by the government in 1620 because it conflicted with the interests of the plantation owners in Virginia. However, it was a very popular crop with the small-scale producer because, although it required a high level of labour from the family, it did not necessitate a large capital outlay. As it was estimated to give a high return of some £40 an acre, tobacco continued to be grown on hundreds of small farms all over the country well into the eighteenth century. Dairy farming was another activity particularly well suited to the small-scale producer. It required only modest capital outlay, could be managed with only family labour and brought a regular income. Areas such as Wiltshire and Cheshire became specialist dairying counties, and several other regions became famed for the cheeses they produced.

## c) Specialist Agricultural Regions

During the seventeenth century there was a considerable increase in specialist agricultural regions. More commercialisation and specialisation meant that family self-sufficiency was gradually being replaced by much greater market orientation, and fewer of the smallholders were general farmers trying to grow all the foodstuffs needed for family consumption. In the same way the various regions of the country were also ceasing to produce all types of food, and were having to import many basic requirements from other areas. The main agricultural division can be defined by a line running from Newcastle in the north-east to Exmouth in the south-west. North and west of this line is the highland zone, which mainly has cool temperatures, high rainfall and thin soils. The lowland areas to the south and east of the line are warmer, have less rain and the soils are deeper. Broadly speaking the highland zone is more suitable for pastoral farming, while the lowlands are better for arable cultivation. The lighter chalk soils of East Anglia were prime areas for cereal production. The downlands and Cotswolds were the fielden, 'sheep-corn' country, which could be used for mixed arable farming and for grazing sheep, which provided valuable manure. In contrast the heavier, moister soils of the Midlands, stretching from Yorkshire down to Wiltshire, were the wood-pasture regions suitable for dairying, stock breeding and pastoral farming. However, there are great variations between regions throughout the country depending on the underlying geology and type of soil. While north-west Norfolk was arable, the south-east of the county was wood-pasture. The Vale of the White Horse in Berkshire had a variety of regions in the small area of some 20 square miles. The east was arable, the north and west were fielden, the south was downland, and the extreme south-west was wood-pasture. Regional specialisation was part of an emerging, interlocking national market, but was dependent on progress towards an improved communication system to allow the quicker circulation of goods (see page 87).

## d) The Consolidation of Specialist Farming

Until the middle of the century both large- and small-scale farming operations continued to prosper. Larger commercial farmers, with higher cash reserves, supplied foodstuffs to the longer-distance London and other urban markets. Although this meant greater transport costs, and a delay in returns, prices were higher (see page 87). Most husbandmen, in contrast, tended to supply local markets, which reduced transport costs and brought quick returns but with lower prices. The continued rise in population and prices ensured profit margins without too much expensive investment. However, this did not mean that even the smaller husbandmen were not responding to the need to grow new crops and improve their techniques. Inventories clearly show that in quite remote rural areas horses were replacing the less efficient oxen - even if two neighbours had to share a horse between them. Considerable interest was shown in woodland management and coppicing to supply the building trade and the expanding ship construction industry. Barley was being grown more widely to supply the maltsters and brewers. Increasingly husbandmen were cultivating small plots of tobacco, hemp, flax, oil seed rape and other industrial crops to supply local needs.

## e) The Spread of the Large Farm

This situation changed after the 1650s when population and inflation levels began to stagnate and wages began to increase. To some extent this did not affect the smallholder using family labour too badly. However, commercial growers using hired labour were doubly squeezed by falling prices and rising wages. The situation was made worse by the disruption caused by the Civil War and many of the lesser gentry and yeomen had to sell their estates (see page 94). This enabled the aristocracy and greater gentry to consolidate their control of land ownership. In a deflationary period estate owners were anxious to preserve their rents and profits in order to maintain their standard of living. Profit levels were protected by the use of enclosure and the adoption of more efficient commercial methods to raise output. At the same time many smaller holdings were amalgamated to create larger farms, which were leased to tenants who could afford to pay higher rents. These tenants in turn had to adopt improved methods so that they made sufficient profit to pay their enhanced rent. Many husbandmen were forced off the land because they could not afford to pay for the improvements that would have enabled them to continue to rent their farms. By the beginning of the eighteenth century a trend towards fewer but larger farms was already established. The agricultural sector was becoming increasingly specialised and oriented towards the national market (see page 87).

## 4 Changing Attitudes Towards Industry

Industrial advances, like those in agriculture, were based on already well established principles. It is now considered that any expansion was not caused by a dramatic increase in production, but rather by a response to a steady rise in demand. At the same time it is thought that the impetus came from the low-cost rural craft trades rather than from the more capital-intensive, heavy industries, such as mining. Manufacturers were having to respond to the same forces affecting landowners and farmers. The deflationary situation after the 1650s, by squeezing profit margins, forced producers to adopt more efficient methods. Similarly, changing patterns of demand at home and abroad put pressure on some of the old traditional manufacturing, while encouraging the introduction of new industries and the expansion of others. Development was sporadic and uneven, but there was greater co-operation between rural and urban industries to supply a national and international market based on London (see page 87).

### a) Patents, Monopolies and Projects

Stuart governments continued the Tudor policy of encouraging economic diversification through the issuing of patents and monopolies. During the seventeenth century these became known as projects, and ranged from the making of tobacco-pipes and pins to financing alum extraction and salt evaporation. The motive remained to encourage the manufacture of goods for the home market and the production of raw materials so as to reduce imports from the continent. However, even under Elizabeth I the system had fallen into disrepute. Many patents were given to courtiers and speculators for financial purposes, rather than to craftsmen to introduce new techniques and create employment. The reason for this was a clash of interests between producers and London importers, because as domestic production rose so imports from the continent fell. This meant that the importers lost money, and because they were influential, they were able to lobby the government. At the same time, as the volume of imports from the continent decreased, government revenue from customs duties went down. To overcome these problems patents were given to those with wealth and City interests who could offer the government a percentage of the profits to offset loss of income from customs. Because of the opposition to this policy from outside London, many of these monopolies were abolished in 1601, but the practice was resumed by James I. During the early seventeenth century London manufacturers with a common interest often formed a consortium, and took out patents which gave them a monopoly so that they could control the industry in the provinces. It was such practices that caused so much debate over monopolies and the rights of free trade up to the Civil War, and to the abolition of many monopolies after the defeat of Charles I. *?*  *1641*

The cause of much of the outcry was that the influential monopolists, unlike the craftsman patentee, were able to enforce their monopolies. The consortia and wealthy speculators could afford to send their agents all over the country to search out and restrict competition. However, this was true only up to a point. The larger manufacturers in the provincial towns were relatively easy to locate, but it was much more difficult to find the small independent producers in the countryside. Consequently, a multiplicity of new industrial processes spread rapidly all over the country as journeymen and day labourers, having learned a new technique, left to set themselves up as independent craftsmen. The effect of this was to promote the growth of rural industry at the expense of many of the provincial towns, which had to develop a new role for themselves (see page 56). This process was helped because most of the expanding industries, such as hat, pin, pottery, and nail making, did not require a large capital outlay, or even workshops and expensive tools.

Individuals and families could operate successfully in cottages and back yards, selling the product for cash in the local market, and using part of proceeds to buy more raw materials. More ambitious individuals might set up small workshops and employ a few day labourers. On an increased scale, entrepreneurs with more capital could establish a putting-out system employing wives and children working in their cottages. As output was larger, the product could be sold to towns and other more distant markets for higher prices. This style of organisation was common in many trades, particularly textiles and glove making. Such operations generally escaped the attention of the monopolists, and so were able to proliferate with little or no restriction.

## b) Rural Industry

The spread of rural industry was helped by a change of attitudes by the authorities. Tudor governments had consistently tried to limit industries to the towns, and to enforce the regulations that anyone operating or employed in a craft industry should have served a seven-year apprenticeship. These restrictions were enforced through the Statute of Artificers of 1563 and other allied legislation. The main purpose of such laws was to maintain the quality and standard of manufactures so that they could be sold abroad. Alongside this viewpoint was the idea that the rural lower orders should be safeguarding 'tillage' by working in arable farming and producing the grain needed to feed the nation. This was all part of the paternalistic view that saw change as a threat to the social structure and the welfare of the nation. Such ideas did not alter overnight and many lingered on well into the seventeenth century, but there were some significant shifts in emphasis. In any case the legislation had little effect because it was very difficult to enforce. By the 1650s the government had begun to see the benefits of the domestic rural industries. Less emphasis was placed on the paramount importance of overseas trade and more attention was paid to full employment and home production. In 1652 the economist Henry Robinson was urging the improvement of rivers and the building of canals to help communications, and by 1674 Carew Robinson was stressing the need to expand domestic industry. Entry into crafts and trades was made much easier by removing the restrictions concerning apprenticeship. The lower orders were no longer being seen as a threat to social stability if they were not usefully employed in agriculture. They were being thought of more as an adaptable labour force adding to national prosperity.

This change of view was closely linked with attitudes towards the quality and sale of goods. Tudor support for urban craft guilds and apprenticeship had been to ensure that manufactures were of a sufficiently high standard to sell abroad. Goods produced by rural industries were generally of non-standard shapes and sizes, and of variable quality and cost. The authorities came to realise that these wide variations were a great advantage in the home market because it gave people at all levels of society the chance to buy what they wanted at a price they could afford. At the same time it was apparent that there was a rising demand for cheaper English goods abroad. In any case, attempts to enforce the regulations had led to trade depressions in the 1620s and 1640s. The result was that the authorities stopped trying to regulate rural industries, which were allowed to produce goods of an increasingly wide range of prices and qualities to meet consumer choice. This led to the emergence of a two-tier industrial structure. Expensive, high quality goods, such as gold and silver ware, jewellery, parchment, clocks, watches and nautical or scientific instruments continued to be produced in the towns for the luxury market. Cheaper goods were made by rural craftsmen to supply the more popular demand. This had a beneficial effect, because urban and rural industries were no longer in competition. Instead, they came to form a symbiotic relationship, with the towns taking over the marketing and distribution of the goods produced in their immediate locality. Sheffield is a good example of this new economic balance. High quality iron and steel wares continued to be made by the town craftsmen, while the cheaper metalwares were produced in the surrounding countryside. Each village tended to specialise in particular items, such as knives, sickles, hoe blades or spades, all of which were in high demand in the colonies.

## 5 Domestic Rural Industries

Such changes in governmental attitudes helped to promote the expansion of rural industry, which had a number of beneficial results. As most of them were labour intensive they provided increasing employment for the lower orders. Much of the labour surplus created by population expansion up to the 1640s and falling employment in agriculture was absorbed by the end of the century. The marked changed in demographic distribution caused by migration (see page 31) was to large extent the result of the better employment prospects of the wood-pasture areas in the Midlands and north of England. The expansion of the metalware trades around Birmingham, Dudley, Wolverhampton, and in Shropshire provided good employment prospects in those areas, especially as population stagnated after the 1640s. At the same time these areas offered a chance of settlement with access to common land and alternative employment in farming, stock raising, fishing, forestry and a range of other activities. It was this opportunity to engage in the dual economy in these open parishes that was so attractive to many migrants. Furthermore, because of the fluidity of the workforce, wages were governed by supply and demand rather than being fixed by regulation. This meant that potentially family incomes were much higher than for those living in the closed fielden parishes where agricultural wages were lower and opportunities for by-employment few.

However, even in the fielden parishes many of the new or improved trades in rural industry were taken up by the overseers of the poor for use in workhouses and the employment of pauper apprentices. All these developments helped to increase family incomes among the lower orders, particularly as wages were rising after the 1650s. This, in turn, increased spending power which by adding to demand encouraged further industrial expansion.

## a) Textiles

Textiles and their allied trades remained the dominant English industry in the seventeenth century especially in East Anglia. From the 1550s Norwich and Colchester had become the main centres of the 'new draperies'. Both towns had benefited from the settlement in East Anglia of Protestant refugees from the Netherlands, and by the early seventeenth century they had some 4,000 immigrant craftsmen. The manufacture, finishing and dyeing of the new, light worsteds, bays, and says was under the control of the clothiers in the two main centres and a few neighbouring towns. In addition, Norwich 'stuffs' were made from various mixtures of wool, silk, cotton and linen which were also much lighter in weight than the woollen cloth of the earlier 'old draperies'. The expansion of the industry provided increased employment in the surrounding countryside. This was controlled by the clothiers and their agents. The preparation of raw materials, the spinning of the yarns, and some of the weaving was carried out in cottages in hundreds of the surrounding villages and small towns. The spinning was the work of the women and children who were poorly paid at 2d or 3d a day. With the decline of the old textile industries in Suffolk and Essex after the 1620s spinning for the 'new draperies' became the major occupation in these counties. Increasingly the raw materials and dyes used in the industry were being produced in England, but some of the finer wools, the cotton and much of the silk had to be imported. However, silk making at Spittlefields in London, and at Sudbury in Suffolk was expanding.

The 'new draperies' and a variety of other allied textile trades in East Anglia spread rapidly to many other parts of the country during the seventeenth century. The introduction of the Dutch small-ware loom enabled the production of ribbons, tapes and a variety of 'fancy' goods in a range of fabrics. This side of the industry was quickly adopted in Manchester and other centres in Lancashire and Yorkshire. Stocking knitting, using the knitting frame introduced from Holland, was another expanding area of production. Woollen stockings were becoming very popular in England and on the continent. As one person could produce only two stockings a week it was difficult to meet demand. For this reason the technique was taken up in cottages all over the country, and became a major source of employment. At the same time stockings made from fine jersey wool or silk were becoming highly fashionable among the elites. Fine linens, lace, cambrics and lawns were also in great demand, with the elites adopting many Italian and French fashions. This side of the industry was given a further boost after the Edict of Nantes (protecting French Protestants) was revoked in 1685. As a result many French craftsmen fled to England to avoid religious persecution.

At the same time other branches of the textile industry were expanding both in East Anglia and elsewhere in England. Fustians, (a fabric with a cotton weft and a linen warp) which had mainly been made in Chester, spread to East Anglia and then to Lancashire. During the seventeenth century the making of fustians and cotton goods became the major Lancastrian manufacture, largely replacing the sixteenth-century linen industry. This led to the production of cheaper ranges of such items as sheets, napkins, shirts, petticoats and aprons. The increasing importation of calicoes, muslins and other cotton fabrics from the Orient (see page 85), while offering competition also stimulated the Lancastrian producers, who tried to reproduce the new fabrics. One of the successful branches of the old West Country textile industry was Devon serge making, which by the end of the century was producing 50 per cent of the total English exports of that material. Canvas making (from hemp) was another thriving trade, boosted by increasing numbers of naval and merchant ships. The craft was introduced into Ipswich by Breton settlers in the sixteenth century. It subsequently spread to Somerset where flax and hemp were already grown, and by the 1650s Yeovil was producing large quantities of linen and hemp thread. By the end of the seventeenth century English canvas makers had a good reputation for producing sails for small trading vessels and for sailors' hammocks. Hemp was also in great demand for making sacks for use in the grain trade, and was widely used in Staffordshire for producing both sacks and ropes.

## b) The Smaller Craft Industries

The great proliferation of the textile trades helped to stimulate a variety of other crafts. Starch making had been introduced into England from the Netherlands to meet the need created by the popular Elizabethan fashion for elaborate starched ruffs. The process of making starch from wheat bran mixed with alum (a double sulphate of aluminium and potassium) and leaving it to steep in water for a month was widely adopted, and starch makers could be found in towns all over England. This had the effect of turning starch from a luxury commodity to one which could be afforded by the lower orders. There was also a useful by-product, because it was found that the waste bran was good for feeding pigs. Alum was also highly in demand because it was used as a mordant for fixing dyes, which led the government to back a project to mine the mineral in England in order to reduce the cost of importation. Deposits of alum had been found in the East Riding of Yorkshire in 1600 and it was planned to extract the 1,000 tons a year used by English industry. However, it proved to be a costly venture and by 1612 investment costs had reached over £36,000, and the yearly production of 600 tons cost over £4 a ton more than it would have done to import it. Although extraction levels rose after the 1630s, this was one of many high-capital ventures that failed to meet expectations during this period.

One industry that attracted successful low-cost projects to improve the quality of its products was pin making. Previously good quality iron and brass pins of all varieties had to be imported from Holland. Costing between 9d and 1s 6d a thousand some £40,000 worth of pins had been imported in 1597. Large quantities of poor quality hand-made pins were already being manufactured in England, especially in the Forest of Dean, from home-produced iron and brass wire. During the sixteenth century the use of superior brass wire imported from Scandinavia had brought some improvement, but finishing remained poor. In the seventeenth century Dutch immigrants introduced new techniques, which revolutionised English pin making. Instead of each pin being produced by one individual, a division of labour was used. Pin shafts and heads being made separately, with the putting together and the sharpening of the pin being the final stages of manufacture. While improving the standard of pins and greatly increasing the volume of production, this also created higher levels of employment. The trade was particularly suitable for children and the disabled, and, following the Dutch example, was widely used in workhouses. The new techniques spread all over the country, but particularly in the Forest of Dean and neighbouring Gloucestershire, with centres at Gloucester, Berkley and Bristol. By the 1630s, despite considerable competition, the

English pin industry was rivalling the Dutch. The success of pin making encouraged the metal crafts and other trades to adopt the practice of a division of labour previously only used widely in the textile industry. Adam Smith, the Scottish political economist, writing *The Wealth of Nations* in 1776 applauding the division of labour and the great development of domestic industry made over the previous hundred years or so, particularly selected the pin industry as the prime example of such progress.

## c) Other Craft Industries

Similar, if less spectacular, headway was made in a whole range of other crafts and trades outside the cloth making and allied sectors. The building, metalwork and leather trades probably employed as many, if not more, people than textiles, but this is hidden by lack of documentation. Building work was a constant source of employment throughout the country. Almost every village had carpenters, glaziers, plumbers and joiners. These crafts often formed part of the dual economy as by-employment for yeomen and husbandmen. During the seventeenth century there was an expansion in building industry as the late Tudor 'great rebuilding' of the mansions and palaces of the elites, especially in the South, spread to the remainder of the country. Moreover, as can be seen from inventories, many yeomen and husbandmen were building new farmhouses, or renovating and adding rooms to their existing houses. Similarly, urban expansion, rebuilding after serious fires in many towns besides London, and the growing aspirations of the pseudo-gentry for stone and brick houses (see page 142), provided ever increasing employment for both skilled and unskilled workers. New trades and professions, such as architects, surveyors, bricklayers, tilers, plasterers, and cabinet and furniture makers, were stimulated by the demand for well designed, comfortable housing with more rooms and greater privacy.

## d) The Leather Trades

For much the same reasons leather goods were greatly in demand. This, along with the increasing market for meat and dairy produce, provided the stimulus for stock raising in the wood-pasture regions. Because of their proximity to the areas of animal husbandry, the Midlands became a major centre of the leather industry. Birmingham, Leicester and Northampton had a wide variety of crafts, ranging from tanning to the making of boots, shoes, bottles, powder flasks, belts, scabbards, harness, gloves, jackets, upholstery, fuses, water pipes, buckets, hinges and bellows. In addition, towns and villages all over the country had their own leather trades in varying numbers. Some towns became specialised, so that in Oxfordshire Burford was a local centre for saddles, while

Woodstock and Charlbury produced a variety of gloves. Apart from the constant underlying need for leather goods, the trade benefited from the changing pattern of demand. The growth in the housing markets meant that not only were more leather goods required for the building trade, but also as part of furnishings of the new houses. Commercialisation in agriculture required a range of new harnesses and other items. Rapidly changing fashions among the elites for leather clothing and accessories were being copied by those lower down the social order. Improvements in transport and travel was a further stimulus generating demand for a vast range of leather items ranging from upholstery for the new travelling coaches, to boots for the cattle being driven from the Scottish borders for fattening by the London butchers.

## e) The Metal Trades

A similar pattern of demand influenced the metal trades. During the seventeenth century Shropshire emerged as a premier area of production. In addition, the towns of Dudley, Wolverhampton, Birmingham and Sheffield developed as specialist centres. However, like the other major trades, metalworking was carried out in towns and villages all over the country to supply local needs. Although there was a rising demand for the watches and clocks, and the gold, silver, pewter, and brass wares produced in London and other major towns for the elite market, this was not the real growth area. The expansion of house and ship building greatly increased the sale of nails, bolts, locks, hinges and other essential items. Improvements in road transport equally produced demand for iron tyres for the new coaches and four-wheel carts. Technological advances in agriculture required the production of a whole new range of tools and equipment. However, the main expansion was in making available a great variety of modestly priced tin or iron ware saucepans, fryingpans, jugs, cups, plates, and cast iron cooking pots and ovens for the lower end of the market. These, along with a variety of cheap trinkets and ornaments, were distributed by peddlers, chapmen and carriers, and by the end the period were on sale in many small back-street shops in the towns.

## 6 Heavy and High Capital-Cost Industries

The success of low-cost investment in the domestic craft trades was rarely matched in other areas of the industrial sector.

## a) The Coal Industry

The coal industry, located in Newcastle, Durham, Yorkshire, the Midlands and Wales, demonstrates some of the difficulties in this sector.

It was once thought (J.U. Nef, *The Rise of the British Coal Industry* (1932)) that coal extraction was a prime example of the 'revolutionary' nature of industrial production in this period. It was calculated that productivity had increased five-fold and that coal was being used extensively as fuel in the brewing, distilling, brick making, malting, and salt evaporation industries. However, despite rising production from all the major centres, coal is now thought to have had less of an impact on the economy than was once claimed. Although coal shipments to London from Newcastle and Durham had reached some 370,000 tons a year by the 1680s and were rising rapidly, it was mainly burned on domestic fires. Very little was being used as industrial fuel. Moreover, the price of coal in London was double that at the pithead, which meant that transport costs made it expensive. For this reason coal was mainly used locally, and new coal-burning industries had to be located close to mining areas. A further problem was that as production rose the more easily worked deposits were exhausted which necessitated deeper mining. This created technical problems with excavating, supporting, and ventilating the new seams, and keeping them free of flooding.

Such work was expensive, and, it was estimated, could cost £1,000 a year. To overcome such difficulties required a considerable injection of capital and additional labour. The high demand from London encouraged greater expenditure in the North East, where some pits had reached a depth of 400 feet by 1700. However, it is doubtful whether other mine owners had a similar incentive. Many of the technical complications were gradually overcome by minor changes rather than by a major break-through. It was not until the end of the century that the main problem of underground flooding was solved. In the 1690s Thomas Savary developed the atmospheric steam pump that was capable of lifting water from considerable depths to replace the less efficient, traditional treadmill pumps powered by horses. However, as the new device required a considerable capital outlay, it was not until well into the eighteenth century that the more efficient pump designed by Thomas Newcomen began to be widely adopted.

## b) The Iron, Lead and Tin Industries

The other major extractive industries - iron ore, lead and tin - faced very similar problems. Iron ore was mined from surface deposits using a shallow, bell-shaped pit. As with coal, increased production led to the more accessible deposits being worked out. Throughout the seventeenth century demand exceeded supply. In any case, much of the ore was of poor quality, which was why the deposits in the Kentish Weald ceased to be used. Because of this, and rising costs, importation of better quality Scandinavian iron increased and had reached 18,000 tons a year by the 1680s. Lead was mined in Derbyshire, the Mendips, the West Riding of Yorkshire and Wales using a traditional technique of extracting lead ore from open trenches. Rising demand for lead for use in the building, printing, paint, shot, pottery and glass industries resulted in the surface deposits being quickly worked out so that it was cheaper to import lead ore from the continent. Similar problems faced the free tin miners in Cornwall, where flooding was especially difficult. Indeed, the industry faced a severe recession until the 1680s because it was cheaper to import tin from the continent than to produce it in Cornwall. It is calculated that there were 12,000 miners in Cornwall and 15,000 in Derbyshire alone in the mid-seventeenth century. Many of these were forced back into farming or other activities within the dual economy because of the difficulties faced by the mining industries.

## c) Smelting

There was more progress on the smelting side of the metal industries, although most of the new technology had been introduced by the late sixteenth century. By the mid-seventeenth century there were 86 of the more efficient charcoal fuelled blast furnaces for iron smelting in operation. These iron works had to be situated near fast-running water so that the bellows for the furnace and the hammer for the forge could be driven by water wheels. They produced iron with a high carbon content which was suitable for cast iron. But the iron had to be reheated and hammered in the forge before it was suitable to make wrought iron goods. Such works were expensive to set up and did not employ much permanent labour, but skilled forge and hammer masters could earn up to £30 a year. Although Abraham Darby, working in Coalbrookdale in Shropshire, was experimenting with using coked coal for smelting to produce cast iron cooking pots from around 1709, it was not until the middle of the century that the new technique was widely exploited. The major break-throughs were in marketing and organisation. During the seventeenth century the Foley family established an iron empire stretching from Yorkshire to the Forest of Dean. By controlling furnaces, mills, forges and warehousing they were able to integrate the processes, and in so-doing made a large fortune. Similar, if less spectacular, progress was made in lead smelting, but, here too, attempts to use coal or peat instead of charcoal in a new reverberatory furnace were not really successful until well into the eighteenth century.

## d) The High Capital-Cost Industries

Many high capital-cost industries that had been introduced in the late sixteenth century made steady progress during the Stuart period. Paper making, sugar refining, tobacco processing, gunpowder manufacture, salt evaporation, and good quality glass and pottery production were all developed from techniques adopted from the continent or brought into the country by refugee craftsmen. Sugar refining and tobacco industries in London, Bristol and Liverpool still catered for a largely luxury market, although judging by the expansion in clay pipe production, smoking was a rapidly growing habit. The number of paper mills using rags and linen to produce white and brown paper was certainly increasing by 1700. The technique of manufacturing gunpowder from saltpetre had been introduced in 1561 from Germany, and England was normally able to produce enough for its own use by 1700. The manufacture of good quality glassware, and particularly of larger panes of window glass was well established. England was also becoming largely self-sufficient in salt. Production from the new brick- and metal-lined salt pans in Northumberland, which used coal-fired furnaces to evaporate seawater fed in through lead pipes, was increasing and becoming competitive with continental suppliers. Commercial pottery production was becoming established around Burslem in Staffordshire and was supplying a wide range of wares for the popular end of the market. But, here again, it was not until the eighteenth century that the Staffordshire potteries really expanded. Pottery making remained largely a small-scale craft industry throughout the seventeenth century. These industries did not have a marked influence on the economy by producing goods for export, and their impact on employment was negligible because they required a small, skilled workforce. However, as in many other industrial areas they were supplying the domestic market, and thus reducing reliance on imports.

## 7 Conclusion

To assess the success or failure of Stuart agriculture and industry it is necessary to reconsider the indicators of economic progress. Agriculture had certainly become more specialised and productive. England was producing enough grain to feed the population and for export in good years. At the same time a much greater variety of foodstuffs was being grown, as well as a range of raw materials for use in industry. Because of greater efficiency there was increased per capita output and this was allowing a transfer of labour into other areas of the economy. However, this must be balanced against the stagnation in population levels after the 1640s which placed less strain on agriculture. It is also possible to argue that much of the transfer of labour represented the absorption of the previously unemployed surplus created by population growth. Considerable expansion appears to have taken place in the domestic craft trades, which produced an increasingly wide range of competitively priced goods. At the same time they provided greater employment prospects, although this is difficult to quantify because so many people were engaged in the dual economy. As in the case of agriculture, the real success of the domestic trades was that not only did they produce enough to supply an increasing demand in the home market, but they also were able to manufacture for export. This is demonstrated by looking at trade figures from London in the 1550s and the 1660s, although it is important to remember that one may not be comparing like with like. Even by the 1660s England was exporting some 53 per cent of the foodstuffs and agricultural raw materials that were being imported a hundred years before. Moreover, England was beginning to export manufactured goods that she had previously had to import.

The heavy and high capital-cost industries could not match this performance, but firm foundations had been laid for expansion in the eighteenth century. However, agriculture and industry cannot be looked at in isolation. Marketing, finance and communications all formed an essential part of the development of the Stuart economy. These issues will be examined in the context of the home market and overseas trade in the chapter 4.

---

**Making notes on** *'The Economy: The Agricultural and Industrial Sectors'*

The first section examines the general state of the English economy in 1600 and the ways that historians measure signs of change. Note carefully how the deficiencies of the sources and data used to analyse the Stuart economy make it difficult to establish an accurate picture of economic developments. Section 2 assesses the problems facing the late Tudor economy and how these continued until the 1640s. Make careful notes on the major reasons for the basic deficiencies of the economy. This section then looks at how the economy began to change after the 1640s. Note in detail how and why the former weaknesses were beginning to be overcome. Section 3 assesses developments in agriculture. You need to weigh-up very carefully the development and advances, and decide which were the most important in enabling England to produce a food surplus after the 1660s. Section 4 assesses how government policies and attitudes about industry changed during the seventeenth century. Make careful notes about these changes and decide which you think were most important in bringing about industrial expansion after the 1650s. The last two sections look at changes in Stuart industry. Make detailed notes about how the different types of industry developed before deciding whether Stuart industrial expansion depended on the more traditional rural and craft industries, or on heavy industry and the new high capital-cost industries.

---

**Source-based questions on** *'The Economy: The Agricultural and Industrial Sectors'*

**1 Changing Attitudes Towards Enclosure**
Carefully read the extracts on page 49. Answer the following questions.
a) Using evidence from the first extract, explain fully why Cecil is

opposed to enclosure. (5 marks)
b) Using evidence from the second extract, explain fully why its author is in favour of enclosure. (5 marks)
c) Compare and contrast Cecil's reasons for opposing enclosures with 'the common objections hitherto raised against inclosures' referred to in the second extract. (4 marks)
d) Compare and contrast the attitudes and values displayed in the two extracts. (6 marks)

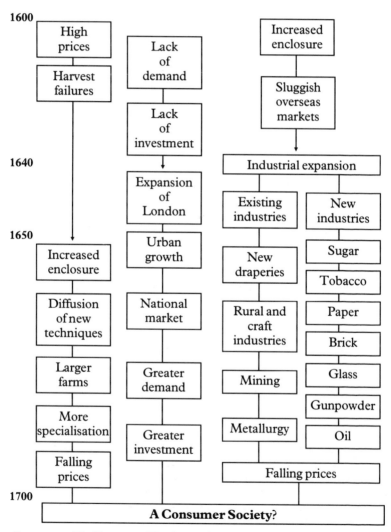

*Summary - The Economy: The Agricultural and Industrial Sectors*

# CHAPTER 4

# The Economy: Overseas Trade, London and the Metropolitan Market

## 1 Introduction: Issues and Approaches

The development of English overseas trade during the seventeenth century had a considerable impact on the country's economic growth. However, there is still no real agreement on whether it was more important to the economy than the domestic market, agriculture, or industry. To some extent the volume of overseas trade is much easier to quantify through government and port authority records than is the case for any other part of the economy. Even so, such evidence is not very reliable before 1700 (see page 42), and really can be used to identify broad trends only. Nevertheless, until comparatively recently, many historians saw the spectacular changes in the pattern of overseas trade as the most significant cause of economic expansion. A major reason for this was the preoccupation with trying to account for the Industrial Revolution (see page 2). The development of world trade was seen as one of the necessary stages towards English industrialisation. The 'commercial revolution' of the seventeenth century was thought to have financed the agricultural revolution of the eighteenth century, which, in turn, paved the way for the Industrial Revolution. Although this approach is now out of favour (see page 11), there was a very strong link between all aspects of the economy, and it is the nature of these connections that economic historians are currently investigating.

### a) Mercantilism

In theoretical terms the seventeenth century has been called the 'age of mercantilism'. This is a concept used in various ways by both modern historians and seventeenth-century political thinkers. The basic notion of mercantilism was created by the political economist Adam Smith when writing in 1776 to describe the economic system of regulation and government control that had been in existence for the previous 200 years. He was advocating a policy of much greater freedom for the individual to trade and for the relaxation of government intervention. In its simplest form the concept of mercantilism was the perception by governments of the need to secure wealth in the form of bullion by creating a favourable balance of trade abroad. Colonies were seen as important possessions which could supply cheap raw materials and provide a market for goods manufactured in the mother country. For this reason they had to be jealously guarded against intervention from other countries. As it was thought in the seventeenth century that market demand was finite and inelastic, the only way that a country could increase its share of the world market was by taking trade away from one of its competitors. A greater share of world trade was seen as essential by leading Western European countries. This led to growing government intervention and increasingly expensive commercial and colonial wars between England, Holland, Spain and France.

Such notions have been developed by some modern historians into elaborate general theories. One of these is the concept of a 'world system' based on the core states of England, France and Holland (see page 6). This is a refinement of Marxist theory which links the rise of capitalism with the development of world trade. The other major theory is that of 'mercantilism', which proposes that the leading western governments had well-planned economic policies to promote mercantilist ideals. Such strategies were thought to have been based on the principle of 'peace, power and plenty'. This meant that to be economically successful a country had to have a strong enough government to impose and enforce economic legislation, maintain peace at home, and to adopt an aggressive policy abroad. The prevention of riot and rebellion allowed the peaceful domestic economy to develop and expand. This enabled the country to produce all the food and manufactured goods for its own needs without having to rely on foreign imports. Hopefully, in addition, domestic output was sufficient to create a surplus which could be exported. The achievement of these objectives created a favourable balance of trade and an inflow of bullion which promoted wealth and plenty. To reach and maintain such a position a nation had to use its power to fight commercial and colonial wars in order to increase its share of the world market. Neither of these theories are now widely accepted because it is felt that they suggest a level of sophisticated central organisation that was beyond the scope of early modern governments. Much of the commercial legislation was more a matter of short-term expedients to meet particular circumstances than of co-ordinated planning.

## b) Contemporary Attitudes Towards Commerce

This is not to say that Stuart governments and political economists did not think along such lines and attach great importance to overseas commerce. The aim was certainly to encourage domestic production and reduce imports so as to improve the balance of trade. The need for such policies had been stressed already by Sir Thomas Smith writing in the 1580s (see page 47). He advocated the production of more foodstuffs and manufactured goods which would not only reduce imports but would also increase employment. Late Tudor governments had adopted measures aimed at achieving these ends through regulation. The patent system combined with poor law and labour legislation had attempted to address the problem of an adverse trade balance and high unemployment. Unfortunately such measures had done little to solve the underlying economic dilemma of producing saleable goods and finding markets in which to sell them. Indeed, attempts to regulate domestic manufacturing to meet the perceived standards required by foreign buyers may well have been detrimental to the home industry. In any case Tudor governments lacked the resources and power to enforce economic policies fully at home or abroad.

Even so, political economists continued to attach great importance to finding new markets abroad. Thomas Mun was an influential figure who was on the board of the East India Company and moved in government circles. In 1622 he published *English Treasure by Foreign Trade* in which he emphasised the need to continue to regulate industry and trade and to find new markets abroad. This meant taking existing markets away from commercial rivals. The book was republished later in the century and continued to influence economic thinking. At the same time the need to defend the expanding English colonies increased the amount of regulation after the 1650s through the passing of Navigation Acts and other protectionist legislation (see page 76). However, although considerable importance was being attached to foreign trade, a much greater realisation of the significance of the domestic market was beginning to become apparent. More writers were stressing the need to encourage demand for English manufactures at home and abroad. A result of this was that much of the restrictive legislation imposed on industry by the Tudor and early Stuart governments gradually ceased to be enforced. By 1728 Daniel Defoe in *A Plan of English Commerce* was commenting that the way of expanding overseas trade was 'the finding out some market for the sale or vent of merchandise, where there was no sale or vent before'. Although this sounds very similar to previous ideas, Defoe was advocating a search for totally new markets, and not just expanding English trade by gaining a greater share of those that already existed. Such thinking was another step towards the Adam Smith concept of free trade for individuals unimpeded by monopoly and regulation.

## c) Economic Growth

Now that general theories are regarded with suspicion, economic historians are more concerned to decide what created economic growth. To establish this it is necessary to discover the exact inter-relationship between overseas trade, agriculture, domestic industry and market forces. What is becoming clearer is that although the economy as a whole was not markedly different to what it had been in the sixteenth century, by the end of the seventeenth century it was beginning to expand. Clearly overseas trade played an important, but not necessarily a paramount, part in such progress. Under the Stuarts the performance of both agriculture and industry began to improve for various reasons (see chapter 3). At the same time there was a considerable expansion in world trade. The question to be decided is in what way interaction between each sector helped to produce such a development. A major difference between Tudor and Stuart overseas trade was the change from being export-led to becoming import-led (see page 81). This, along with colonial expansion, can be seen as a major stimulus to English industry. Equally it can be argued that the growth of the domestic and world market, improved banking and financial institutions, and the emergence of London as the centre of world trade was even more important. These issues will be discussed in the following sections and comparisons will be made with developments in agriculture and industry.

## 2 Problems of Late Tudor and Early Stuart Trade

Until the middle of the seventeenth century there appeared little real improvement in England's overseas trade performance. In this respect commerce followed a pattern very similar to the industrial and agricultural sectors, but for somewhat different reasons. Stuart overseas trade can be divided into three distinct areas - northern and southern Europe, America and the Atlantic, and the Orient. These zones of interest had already been established in a rudimentary form by 1600. The type of commercial activity varied between the three spheres, and each of them presented its own particular difficulties.

During the late sixteenth century English merchants had already begun to extend their markets within Europe. The collapse of old trade in unfinished textiles to the Netherlands in the 1580s and the development of the 'new draperies' (see page 57) had forced them to seek new commercial outlets. Much of this expansion had been based on the creation of joint stock companies which gave groups of London merchants the monopoly of trade in certain areas under royal charter. The earliest of these ventures was undertaken by a group of London merchants who formed the Muscovy Company in 1555 to trade with Russia and the Baltic. English cloth was exchanged for furs, amber, pitch, tar, timber and other ship building materials. Company officials also tried unsuccessfully to open up an overland trade with Asia through Persia. At the same time merchants from Bristol and other south-western ports established new commercial links with the Netherlands, Calais and Cadiz, and began trading cloth for gold and ivory along the West African coast. Simultaneously traders from east coast ports, such as Newcastle and Hull, began trading with the Baltic, Scandinavia and Iceland. In 1579 a group of London merchants formed the Levant Company to trade with Turkey and the Mediterranean. They exchanged cloth for spices, silk and oils brought from Asia along the overland trade routes. Like the Muscovy Company they sent officials to try to open up direct trade with the East and by 1591 English adventurers had reached as far as Burma and Siam.

However, by the 1590s the whole of Europe was suffering from a trade recession brought about by over-population, inflation and exhaustion from the long series of dynastic and religious wars. Commerce remained depressed until the middle of the seventeenth century. The situation was made worse by the crippling effects of the Thirty Years War which began in 1618 in Germany and eventually drew in all the major continental states. England, while not being directly involved, suffered from the effects of ineffective government, loss of trade, and over-regulation in industry (see page 55). These conditions all combined to cause severe depressions in the 1620s and 1630s and were followed by the disruption of civil war in the 1640s.

## 3 America, the Caribbean and the Far East

### a) Tudor Colonisation in the Americas

Although there had been an expansion of English commercial outlets in Europe, there had been little real progress breaking into Atlantic trade and the New World by 1600. Sebastian Cabot, a Venetian explorer sponsored by Bristol merchants, had reached Newfoundland in 1497. But no attempt had been made to follow up this discovery both through fear of infringing Spain's monopoly of the New World and because of a lack of interest in the cod fisheries by the government and London merchants. However, some interest in the Atlantic was shown by traders from the south-western ports despite opposition from London. The most noteable ventures were carried out by William Hawkins, who, sailing from Plymouth in the 1520s and 1540s, traded in pepper and ivory along the West African coast and crossed the Atlantic to Brazil and the Caribbean.

Even so, it was not until after 1558, when English relations with Spain began to deteriorate, that interest in Atlantic trading became significant. In 1562 William Hawkins's son John tried to break the Spanish monopoly of trading slaves from West Africa to supply labour for their colonies in South America and the West Indies. He successfully exchanged 300 slaves from Senegal with Spanish colonists in Hispaniola in return for sugar, hides and gold. But on a third expedition accompanied by Francis Drake in 1567 his ships were trapped and most were destroyed by a Spanish squadron at San Juan de Ulloa in Mexico. While this temporarily restored the Spanish monopoly, a basis had been laid for English domination of the highly lucrative 'triangular trade' in the late seventeenth century (see page 84). This disaster encouraged Hawkins and Drake along with a number of English merchants to turn to privateering (sailing with letters of marque from the monarch empowering them to attack enemy ships) in Spanish America and the

Caribbean. These activities culminated in Drake circumnavigating the world between 1577 and 1580. Not only had he broken the Spanish monopoly of the sea routes around the Cape of Good Hope and Cape Horn, but he also brought back six tons of cloves from the East Indies worth £1.5 million. Here again this was largely an isolated success. At the same time attempts were being made to find a north-west sea route to the East which would avoid antagonising Spain. In the 1570s Sir Humphrey Gilbert organised voyages to Baffin Island and Hudson Bay to find a possible sea passage (see map, page 82). Early hopes of success led to the formation of the Company of Cathay but the project ended in financial disaster. Further attempts by John Davis in the same area met with similar failure.

Growing hostility towards Spain in the 1580s led to further efforts to establish English influence in the New World. Richard Hakluyt's *Principal Navigations,* written in the 1580s, extolled the advantages of exploration and the use of seapower and colonisation to provide new markets and sources of raw materials. In 1583 Sir Humphrey Gilbert took 200 colonists to Newfoundland and Novia Scotia. Although he claimed Newfoundland for England, the scheme collapsed when the ships sailing from Nova Scotia were wrecked, and Gilbert was drowned, on the return voyage to England. Other attempts at colonisation proved equally unsuccessful. Sir Walter Raleigh's scheme to colonise the area of modern Virginia met with two failures. The first attempt in 1584, led by Sir Richard Grenville with ten ships, had to be abandoned in 1587 because the colonists could not adapt to the conditions and quarrelled with local Indians. A second expedition led by John White tried to re-establish the settlement in 1587. White returned to England for fresh supplies, but he was delayed by the Armada campaign, and found the site totally abandoned on his return in 1591. Although the defeat of the Armada had given England temporary control of the seas the Tudors made no further attempts at colonisation in the Americas.

## b) Stuart American Colonisation

Even so the experience gained from these misadventures soon led to renewed interest in colonisation after the accession of James I. The Virginia Company was chartered by the king to re-establish settlement in the area previously proposed by Raleigh. In 1607 they sponsored an expedition by 120 adventurers whose primary objective was to search for gold rather than to establish a colony. They landed in Chesapeake Bay, but were immediately attacked by Indians, and built a fort on an unhealthy, swampy site on the James River. The search for gold was unsuccessful, and 80 of the original party died from disease and Indian attacks within the first year. However, although poorly positioned and prone to disease, Jamestown quickly began to attract numbers of settlers. By 1610 900 settlers, including women and children, had arrived and had begun farming and fishing, but disease and Indian attacks had reduced numbers to 150 a year later. Despite setbacks from disease and Indian wars, the colony survived supported by a constant flow of new settlers. The Virginia Company appointed a Governor in 1611 and the farmers began to grow tobacco, sending the first consignment of 20,000 pounds to England in 1613. Tobacco was to become a major item of English colonial trade during the seventeenth century (see page 85). Many members of the landed and urban elites, or their sons, were attracted to the colony because of the high profits to be made from tobacco. They established large plantations which were at first worked by indentured servants, vagrants, orphans and convicts brought in from England. Later the plantation owners began to use black slave labour from West Africa (see page 83). In 1632 Charles I granted an adjacent tract of land to Lord Baltimore who founded the colony of Maryland for Catholic refugees. The land proved very suitable for tobacco growing and colony quickly attracted settlers and plantation owners.

Meanwhile, to the north, other English settlements were being created. In November 1620 the Mayflower arrived off Cape Cod with 101 settlers. Half of these colonists were Puritans fleeing from religious persecution in England. The remainder had been expecting to go to Virginia, but finally they all signed the 'Mayflower Compact' agreeing to keep 'just and equal lawes' as agreed by the whole colony. They established a settlement at Plymouth in New England. Unlike the first settlers at Jamestown they had no problem with the local Indians. However, they found survival in the wilderness equally hard and half the colonists had died by the end of the first winter. Even so new settlers arrived. By 1628 the Massachusetts Bay Company had been formed, largely under Puritan control, and had been granted extensive land rights. The area became a haven for Puritan religious refugees and by 1643 the population had reached 1,600. During the 1630s other colonies were established at Maine and Rhode Island, again mainly settled by religious refugees. In contrast to the colonies to the south, New England was not suitable for the cultivation of tobacco and so was not attractive to plantation owners. For this reason the northern colonies developed as more equalitarian communities of small farmers and traders and had a different economy from those in the south.

## c) The Caribbean

Apart from sporadic privateering the Tudor adventurers made no real effort to gain a foothold in the Caribbean. Then in the seventeenth century the English, like the French and the Dutch, began to break the Spanish monopoly of the area by occupying islands. Bermuda, isolated well to the north of the other West Indian islands, was settled by 60 English colonists in 1612. St Kitts was occupied by Sir Thomas Warner, his family and 14 other colonists in 1624. They established good relations with the native Indians and began to grow tobacco. By 1625 they had produced 7,000 pounds of tobacco which was sent to England. As a reward Charles I granted Warner rights to the neighbouring islands of Barbados, Nevis and Monserrat. Barbados was colonised in 1627 and attracted some 1,600 settlers within a year. Antigua and other smaller islands in the Leeward group were settled during the 1630s. Control of Antigua gave the English the best natural harbour in the Caribbean. Until 1640 the main crop grown on the islands was tobacco. Then the English settlers began to follow the example of the Dutch colonists who had started to grow sugar cane, which was introduced in the 1630s from Brazil. Sugar was a highly lucrative crop and was to become the major product of the West Indies (see page 81). For this reason the islands, like England's southern mainland colonies, attracted wealthy settlers who established large sugar plantations.

After the Civil War Cromwell planned to use the Commonwealth's increased military and naval power to strengthen English trade. In 1650 and 1651 two Navigation Acts were passed, designed to force the new colonies to transport their raw materials only in English ships. This was to be the foundation of England's supremacy in the carrying trade. Forty new large and heavily gunned war ships were brought into commission during the next three years, which doubled the size of the navy (see page 79). However, the Dutch, who had previously controlled the carrying trade, resented these moves and war broke out. Commanded by two former generals, George Monk and Robert Blake, the English navy won two major sea battles, gained control of the trade routes, and by blockading the coast of Holland forced the Dutch to make peace in 1654.

Encouraged by this success Cromwell decided to take control of the Caribbean away from Spain. The 'western design' was launched in 1655 as a joint military and naval expedition to capture Hispaniola (the largest of the Caribbean islands). However, the campaign was badly co-ordinated and the quality of the troops was poor. As a result the attack on Hispaniola was easily beaten off, but the English did manage to capture Jamaica. Although half the garrison died from disease within six months, the island soon attracted settlers and became a strategic naval base (see page 81). It is estimated that by 1643 about 65,000 people had left England to settle in the American colonies and the West Indies. During the 1640s and 1650s these numbers were increased still further as many people left England to escape the effects of the war and the Interregnum. Cromwell added to the exodus by shipping large numbers of convicts and prisoners of war to the West Indies.

## d) The Far East

Although the defeat of the Armada had no impact on Tudor

colonisation it did promote interest in developing Far Eastern trade and so breaking the Portuguese monopoly. A number of voyages to the East Indies in the 1590s tried to emulate the Dutch in establishing trade, but all met with failure. However, in 1600 a group of 242 London merchants formed the East India Company under royal charter. James Lancaster, who had previous experience in the East Indies, was given command of five ships. The fleet sailed in 1601 taking £30,000 in silver, iron, lead and cloth, which it hoped to exchange for gems, spices, sulphur and camphor. A trading factory (warehouse) was established in Java, and although there was no demand for the cloth, the ships returned in 1603 with merchandise valued at £3 million. In 1604 an English fleet under William Hawkins sailed to Surat in India to try to gain trading concessions from the Mughal emperor Jahangir. Portuguese influence proved too strong at this point, but in 1613 growing English sea power in the Indian Ocean gained the East India Company the right to set up a factory at Surat. However, there were growing difficulties with the Dutch in the East Indies where Company merchants had established several bases. The Dutch aimed to control the spice trade from their main centre at Amboyna in the Moluccas. In 1623 they accused the English of plotting to seize control by assassinating the Dutch governor, and ten English merchants were executed. As a result of the Amboyna 'massacre' the East India Company lost control of trade in the East Indies apart from two factories in Java and Sumatra. These were eventually captured by the Dutch in 1682.

The Company's main interest turned to India, where during the 1630s they established a major base at Madras to control the trade in tea and coffee. The growing fashion for tea and coffee drinking enabled rapid expansion, and by the 1640s they had set up 25 trading posts in India staffed by 100 Company officials at a cost of £5,000 a year. Even so, trading conditions were very difficult until the 1660s. Famines and native wars, as the Mughal empire became increasingly unstable, seriously disrupted trade. The English Civil War caused problems because of the East India Company's close links with the monarchy, which meant that it was distrusted by Parliament and the new Commonwealth. Finally, in 1657, a threat by the Company to abandon Eastern trade altogether led Cromwell to cancel their charter and to issue a new one to a group of rival merchants.

## 4 The Basis of Trade: The Navigation Acts and Sea Power

At the Restoration in 1660 England was in an ideal position to take a leading role in world trade. The country had largely recovered from the disruption of the Civil War. Naval reforms and victory over the Dutch during the Commonwealth period had turned England into a strong sea power. The basis for commercial development had been securely laid in Europe, America and the Caribbean, as well as in India. During the period from 1660 to 1713 England fought a series of successful commercial wars against Holland, France and Spain that were to establish her as the leading commercial power in the eighteenth century. The pattern of trade that emerged developed naturally out of the expertise gained by English merchants over the previous century. However, there were a number of essential differences after 1660. England had a strong enough navy to control the sea routes, enforce the Navigation Acts, and protect English colonies and merchant ships all over the world. The expansion of domestic industry and the easing of government industrial regulation gave English merchants an increasingly wide range of goods to sell abroad in addition to woollen textiles. The development of England's American and Caribbean colonies provided an ever growing source of sugar and tobacco and other cheap raw materials. This not only gave further stimulus to domestic industry but also allowed the development of the highly lucrative re-export trade (see page 86). At the same time East India Company trade, although paid for mainly in silver, brought in large quantities of luxury items, a considerable proportion of which could be profitably re-exported. It was this that converted Stuart commerce into being primarily import rather than export led. The increasing quantities of raw materials and other items being imported into England could be directly re-exported in English ships, partly processed before re-export (for example, raw sugar into molasses), or fully manufactured before sale abroad. In this way merchants profited from the resale of goods at various stages as well as from the invisible earnings of carrying the goods in English ships. At the same time industry benefited from the constant flow of raw materials for manufacturing.

## a) The Navigation Act

In order for this system to operate successfully it was necessary for England to establish naval supremacy and to enforce the navigation laws which had been introduced during the Commonwealth period. The Navigation Act of 1660 as well as confirming the earlier legislation, laid down that goods from foreign countries could be brought to England only in English ships or in those from the country of origin. This legislation, if it could be enforced, would give England complete domination of trade with the colonies, and a considerable share of the carrying trade to other countries. It was this aspect that caused anxiety not only to England's competitors but also to her own colonists.

---

Navigation Act, 1660

1 For the increase of shipping and encouragement of the navigation of this nation wherein, under the good providence and protection

of God, the wealth, safety and strength of this kingdom is so much
concerned; be it enacted ...that from and after the first day of
5 December one thousand six hundred and sixty, and from them
thenceforward, no goods or commodities whatsoever shall be
imported into or exported out of any lands, islands, plantations
[colonies] or territories to his Majesty belonging or in his
possession ... in Asia, Africa or America, in any other ship or ships,
10 vessel or vessels whatsoever, but in ships or vessels as do truly and
without fraud belong only to the people of England ... and whereof
the master and three-fourths of the mariners at least are English.

---

The Humble Remonstrance of John Bland of London, Merchant, on the
behalf of the Inhabitants and Planters of Virginia and Maryland, 1663

1 Most humbly representing unto your Majesty the inevitable
destruction of these colonies, if so be that the late Act for increase
of trade and shipping be not as to them dispensed with ... Virginia
and Maryland are colonies, which though capable of better
5 commodities, yet for the present afford only these, tobacco chiefly,
then in the next place corn and cattle ... if you keep thence the
Hollanders, can it be believed that from England more ships will be
sent than are able to bring thence what tobacco England will spend
[buy] (If the Act is to remain in force) Then let me on the behalf of
10 the said colonies of Virginia and Maryland make these following
proposals ... First, that the traders to Virginia and Maryland from
England shall furnish and supply the planters and inhabitants of
these colonies with all sorts of commodities and necessaries which
they may want or desire, at as cheap rates and prices as the
15 Hollanders used to have ... Secondly, that the said traders out of
England to these colonies shall not only buy of the planters such
tobacco in the colonies as is fit [needed] for England, but take all
that shall be yearly made by them, at as good rates and prices as the
Hollanders used to give.

---

The fears expressed in 1663 were based on the assumption that without
foreign competition the colonies would be unable to sell enough tobacco
and other raw materials to be able to afford all the manufactured goods
they required, and that, in any case, England was incapable of supplying
these cheaply enough. Such fears proved to be unfounded because
England was to develop an almost insatiable demand for raw materials,
and English industry was beginning to produce a wide range of cheap
consumer goods.

The Navigation Act and the associated Staple Act of 1663, which
stipulated that all continental goods destined for the colonies had to first

be sent to England, became the basis for English commercial expansion. England was assured of a constant supply of cheap raw materials from her colonies. This promoted industrial growth and provided a growing volume of goods for the re-export trade. At the same time the colonies provided a protected market for English manufactures. This steadily increased as the colonial population grew and became more wealthy through the export of raw materials. However, before this benign situation could be achieved England had to be able to enforce her monopoly against foreign competition.

## b) The Dutch Wars

In 1660 England's main commercial rival was still Holland. The Dutch maintained their domination of the carrying trade with the Far East and controlled the West African slave trade. They resented both English attempts to break into these areas and the imposition of the Navigation Acts. The Second Dutch War broke out in 1664. England captured New Amsterdam from the Dutch, renaming it New York, so linking the northern and southern English colonies in America. However, after defeating the Dutch fleet at the battle of Lowestoft in 1665, England was disrupted by Great Plague of London and the subsequent fire which destroyed large areas of the capital. Due to shortage of money to pay the sailors and maintain the ships, the English fleet was laid-up at Chatham. It was largely destroyed by the Dutch fleet which broke through the Thames defences in 1666. An uneasy peace ensued until 1672 when England allied with France against Holland. The Third Dutch War was as disastrous as its predecessor. The Anglo-French fleet was defeated at the battle of Texel and England withdrew from a war that had cost £6 million.

## c) The Wars with France

The Glorious Revolution of 1688 and the accession of William of Orange and Mary brought an alliance between England and Holland against France. The war that resulted - the War of the League of Augsburg - began badly with the Anglo-Dutch fleet being defeated off Beachy Head in 1690. This led to a major review of the navy and the opening of new shipbuilding yards at Portsmouth and Plymouth. Two years later the French were defeated at the battle of La Hogue. However, the war proved indecisive and an uneasy peace was made in 1697. When hostilities were resumed in 1702 the navy was in a much better state of preparation. Although this new war - the War of the Spanish Succession - was dominated by land battles, the navy was very successful against French and Spanish colonies and strategic bases. This enabled England to make some significant commercial and colonial gains from the Treaty of Utrecht which ended the war in 1713. Bases captured from Spain at Gibraltar and Minorca strengthened the navy's position in the Mediterranean. French colonial territories in Newfoundland, Nova Scotia and Hudson Bay were all retained. English merchants secured the right to supply slaves to the Spanish American colonies. In addition, Holland, although retaining control of East Indian trade, had been too exhausted by the long wars with France to offer serious competition in England's other spheres of commercial interest.

## d) The Establishment of Naval Supremacy

Another important outcome of these wars was that the navy had gained considerable experience protecting and convoying merchant ships. The main wartime threat to English commerce came from privateers, although the French sometimes used small squadrons of warships as commerce raiders. The area of greatest danger was the English Channel which was used by the majority of merchant ships leaving or entering the port of London. As until 1700 well over half of English commercial shipping was centred on London this was a very sensitive issue. Although the navy had been used to convoy ships from late Middle Ages, the level of expertise was still not very high by the seventeenth century. The main problem was to have enough small warships, frigates and sloops, for convoying, while maintaining sufficient reserves for patrolling and supporting the battle ships in blockade and other duties. The expansion of English merchant shipping from some 100,000 tons in 1600 to nearly 300,000 tons by 1700 only increased the difficulties. During the Dutch wars even the east coast collier fleets had been so heavily attacked that the price of coal in London doubled. French privateers proved equally destructive in the 1690s and 9 warships were stationed in the North Sea and another 50 in the English Channel and Mediterranean. Even so, despite large convoys, many merchant ships were lost, such as the Smyrna convoy to Turkey in 1693 when 200 out of 400 ships were captured by the French. The Admiralty estimated that some 4,000 merchant ships were lost between 1689 and 1697.

In 1696 the Council of Trade was establish to co-ordinate an improved convoy system in consultation with the Admiralty and merchant groups. As a result frigates and sloops were detailed to patrol the coasts, and frigate squadrons were stationed in the North Sea. Fleets of battle ships were sent to the English Channel and the Mediterranean. Smaller squadrons were also set up in Newfoundland, New York, the Caribbean, and the west coast of Africa. Despite this, continued shortages of escort ships and lack of co-ordination meant that Baltic, Mediterranean and West Indian convoys still lost many ships. In 1708 the Convoys and Cruisers Act laid down that a reserve of 43 war ships had to be constantly retained to act as convoy escorts. By 1713 the system was working quite effectively and the Admiralty estimated that the loss of merchant ships had been halved in the War of the Spanish Succession as compared with the shorter War of the League of Augsburg.

## 5 Post-Restoration Commerce

The volume of overseas trade increased throughout the seventeenth century, but the greatest growth came after 1660. The most significant change taking place was the alteration in the balance between trade with continental Europe and that with the rest of the world. It has been estimated (remembering that the figures are approximate and only based on London) that in the 1640s 63 per cent of trade was with

*Title page of* England's Safety *by George St. Lo, a tract of 1693 which appealed for a strengthening of England's naval resources*

northern Europe and 31 per cent with southern Europe and the Mediterranean. By the 1660s northern European trade had fallen to 45 per cent, that with southern Europe remained the same, but the American and Eastern total had risen to 24 per cent. By 1700 trade with Europe and the Mediterranean had fallen to 67 per cent, the remainder coming from America and the East. At the same time the nature of English commerce was also changing with a growing emphasis on imports and the re-export trade. In the 1640s imports were £2.7 million of which £0.5 million were re-exported, while domestic exports totalled £2.3 million. Twenty years later domestic exports had risen to £3 million, but the total of imports had reached £4 million of which £0.9 million were re-exported.

By 1700 the contrast was even greater with domestic exports of £4.4 million, but imports of £5.8 million, of which £2 million were re-exports. This expansion was by no means consistent or continuous. The early seventeenth-century commercial depression appears to have ended by the 1640s. Trade was buoyant until 1660, possibly indicating that the Civil War was less disruptive, and that Cromwell's commercial policy was more successful than has often been suggested. Commercial activity slowed down again during the Dutch wars, but increased until the 1690s. The end of the War of the League of Augsburg brought renewed activity until 1702, when expansion was slowed down by the War of the Spanish Succession. Clearly, although England had succeeded in establishing naval and commercial supremacy and enforcing the Navigation Acts by 1713, it was at the cost of disrupting the very trade that the wars were fought to augment. At the same time warfare had become very expensive, and the additional taxation and duties raised by the government adversely affected investment (see page 89).

## a) The Caribbean and North America

As the new commercial pattern emerged the colonies in America and the Caribbean took on a growing significance. Not only were they a source of valuable raw materials and a growing market for English domestic exports, but they were also an integral part of the highly lucrative 'triangular trade' in slaves. The West Indies were regarded as the most important of the colonies because of their sugar exports. Sugar was in high demand in Europe as a result of the growing fashion for drinking sweetened coffee, chocolate and tea. For this reason strong naval squadrons were stationed at Jamaica and Antigua, and West Indian convoys were heavily protected. Imports of sugar rose from a mere 150 cwts in the 1670s to some 400,000 cwts, worth £630,000, by 1700. Apart from boosting the sugar refineries at Bristol and Liverpool, at least a third of the imports were profitably re-exported as raw sugar or molasses. However, the West Indies were less useful as a market for

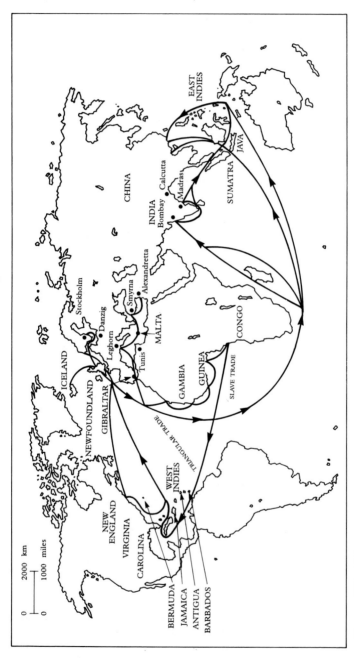

*Stuart World Trade 1603–1714*

English exports because there was no mass market. After the rapid rise in population up to the 1660s - some 40,000 in Jamaica and Barbados alone - the number of white settlers began to decline. Apart from the high death rate from yellow fever and dysentery, the main reason for this was that some 80 per cent of the cultivated land on the islands was used for sugar plantations. This meant that there was little opportunity for small farmers, and, as black slave labour was more efficient and cheaper, fewer convicts and indentured servants were sent from England.

In contrast the white population in the mainland American colonies continued to expand (see page 32) and may have reached half a million by the early eighteenth century. The export of tobacco from the southern colonies increased very rapidly from 20,000 pounds (weight) in 1619 to 1.5 million pounds in 1629. It had reached 22 million pounds by 1700. Once again the west coast ports of Bristol and Liverpool benefited as their tobacco processing industries thrived. Two-thirds of the imported tobacco was re-exported to the continent, at first in its raw state, but increasingly as a manufactured product as the English tobacco industry displaced its Dutch rivals. By the early eighteenth century the southern colonies were beginning to export some raw cotton, and, especially after the settlement of the Carolinas in 1663, increasing quantities of rice. The more northerly colonies were less fortunate in that they were unable to grow any of the raw materials that were in high demand in England. However, the farming communities prospered and expanded, while the coastal towns developed thriving shipbuilding and trading businesses. Fishing was another important industry, which benefited from a rising demand for Newfoundland cod from continental Europe. The Navigation Acts ensured that the expanding mass and luxury market in the American colonies was dependent on English exports. In the 1660s exports from English domestic industry to the colonies had been negligible, but by 1700 they had reached 12 per cent of total domestic exports. The exports covered the whole range of textiles, metal, brass, copper and glass wares, tools, weapons and utensils, as well as fashionable furniture, coaches, and carpets for the wealthy planters. At the same time re-exports to the colonies increased to 16 per cent of the total by 1700. This represented the increasing wealth of the southern colonies, and the demand for the tea, coffee, cottons, silks and spices imported by the East India Company.

## b) The Slave Trade

The development of tobacco and sugar plantations in the southern American and Caribbean colonies increased English interest in the Atlantic slave trade. Until the middle of the seventeenth century the trade had been controlled by the Portuguese and the Dutch. They had established fortified trading stations along the west coast of Africa on sites leased from African chiefs. The slaves were supplied by the local chiefs, who found this a lucrative way of disposing of prisoners of war, convicts and unwanted members of their own tribes. This was part of the 'triangular trade' which was based on the direction of the prevailing Atlantic winds. Trade goods were shipped from Europe to the West African coast and exchanged for slaves. The slaves were then shipped across to the Americas and the Caribbean where they were sold in exchange for sugar and other high-priced commodities, such as mahogany. The ships then returned to Europe where the goods were sold at a considerable profit. Naturally, English merchants were eager to participate in such a remunerative enterprise. In 1663 the Royal Adventurers of England Trading to Africa was set up as a chartered company undertaking to deliver 3,000 slaves a year to the West Indies. To mark English interest in West Africa the mint began to issue the guinea coin made from pure gold from the Guinea coast. Not surprisingly, the Dutch resented this further intrusion into their commercial dominance. Taking advantage of their success in the naval war they captured all but one of the English trading posts in 1667 and the company collapsed with a loss of £120,000. However, in 1672 the Royal African Company was set up and, taking advantage of England's increasing naval supremacy, established new forts and trading posts from Senegal to Angola. It is thought that about 50,000 slaves a year were being shipped to the New World for the rest of the century. In Barbados alone the number of slaves rose from 20,000 in 1650 to 80,000 by 1700. Gaining the right to supply slaves to the Spanish colonies in 1713 strengthened the position of the Royal African Company which soon dominated the West African coast from the Gambia to the Congo. This gave English merchants control of at least 50 per cent of the 'triangular trade', mainly through the ports of Bristol and Liverpool.

## c) The Far East

Although the Dutch continued to control trade with the East Indies, the East India Company established itself firmly in India after 1660. Charles II restored the company's charter and gave it the additional privileges of being able to issue money, maintain a private army to wage war, and to exercise jurisdiction over all English subjects in India. Even so the continuing instability in India meant that the Company needed a strong military base. This problem was solved by the marriage of Charles II to the Portuguese princess, Catherine of Braganza, in 1662, because part of her dowry was the Indian island of Bombay. In 1668, in return for a loan, the king leased Bombay to the Company for an annual rent of £10. They fortified the island and this became one of their major bases in India, along with Calcutta and Madras. There were more problems in England after the deposition of James II because of the Company's close links with the court. In the 1690s William III issued a charter to a rival group of merchants. However, the Indian luxury trade was highly specialised. Commercial agreements had to be carefully negotiated with local princes, and the buyers had to be well in tune with European elite tastes and fashions. English goods did not sell well in India, and so most commodities had to paid for in silver. East India Company ships had to be specially built and heavily armed because of the bullion and the value of the cargoes they carried. For such reasons, by 1708 the rival companies had amalgamated with a capital of £3 million, and an annual turnover of some £700,000. They had a virtual monopoly in supplying Europe with coffee, tea, calicoes (cotton goods), cloves, cinnamon, pepper, silks and Chinese porcelain. By 1700 the total value of Eastern trade had risen to an annual £650,000 and comprised 13 per cent of English imports. Of this total calicoes represented 56 per cent, silks 23 per cent and pepper 16 per cent. By the 1720s imports had reached £900,000, but the distribution had changed. Calicoes at 48 per cent and silks at 22 per cent were still dominant, but pepper had fallen to 2 per cent, while tea and coffee had risen from 1 per cent to 13 per cent. This was a clear indication of the changing tastes of the European and colonial elites. Although the export of bullion to buy these goods was contrary to the principles of the period, the profit margins on the re-export trade were high enough to remove all doubts about the wisdom of trading with India.

## d) Europe

The effect of these developments in the East and the Americas on England's trade with the continent appears to have been small before 1700. The three major trading areas continued to be the Baltic, northern and central Europe, and southern Europe and the Mediterranean. The nature of the commerce remained very similar, with woollen cloth being exchanged for timber and other shipbuilding materials from the Baltic, manufactures from northern Europe, and wines and other luxuries from the Mediterranean countries. By the early eighteenth century the major impact on the commercial pattern was the rising volume of non-European imports, accompanied by a sharp increase in the level of re-exports. In 1700 imports totalled some £5.8 million, 68 per cent of which came from Europe, 13 per cent from the East and 19 per cent from the Americas.

By 1713 the actual volume of imports had fallen slightly to £5.4 million because of the effects of the wars with France. However, the distribution was already shifting. European imports stood at 61 per cent, American imports had risen to 22 per cent, and those from Asia to 17 per cent. That this was the beginning of a lasting trend can be seen by looking at the figures for 1739, when total imports had reached £7.4 million. European imports had fallen to 48 per cent, while those from the Americas had risen to 34 per cent, those from the East remained at

17 per cent, and African imports had risen from 0.2 to 0.5 per cent. Over the same period the trend in exports does not show such a marked change. Between 1700 and 1739 exports rose from £6.4 to £8 million, showing that a favourable trade balance had been achieved by the end of the seventeenth century. The destination of exports remained constant with 80 per cent going to Europe, about 15 per cent going to the Americas, and the remainder going to Africa and Asia. A very important difference was that by 1700 re-exports of both colonial and Eastern imports, which had been a mere 4 per cent of the total in 1650, had risen to 30 per cent and were valued at about £1.1 million.

The rapid expansion of English commerce between 1660 and 1700 did not appear to have had any great influence on the distribution of her trade with Europe. Woollen textiles had begun to lose their former domination. In the 1650s textiles still constituted around 80 per cent of total exports, but by 1713 this figure had fallen to possibly 60 per cent. To some extent this reflected competition from the Dutch cloth industry, except in southern Europe where English textile sales actually rose. This trade gap was being filled by re-exports, for which the continent was becoming increasingly dependent on England because of her growing naval supremacy. At the same time there was a continuing sluggishness in continental demand. For this reason, the increasing diversity in English industry (see page 56) and the growing range of available goods was having no apparent effect on domestic export figures. However, in the period up to 1750, while woollen textile exports continued to decline, and re-exports figures stagnated, domestic exports rose rapidly. This suggests that the industrial changes of the late seventeenth century had laid a firm basis for a continued growth in overseas trade.

## 6 London and the Metropolitan Market

While there was undoubtedly considerable expansion in England's overseas trade, it is generally agreed that the main area of growth in the Stuart economy was in the domestic market. In contrast to the continent there was an increasing level of demand in England because of the rise in the standard of living among all sections of society (see page 35). At the same time changes within the domestic market not only maintained the level of demand, but also helped to facilitate the expansion in overseas trade. It is considered that London was the main 'engine of economic growth' within the system, and that the growth of the London market promoted the extension of services and improvements in communications that was essential for sustained national expansion.

## a) The Growth of London

A major reason for this expansion was London's spectacular demographic growth (see page 33). A population increase from 190,000 in 1600 to 575,000 by 1700 made it the largest city in Western Europe and the major centre of demand for consumer goods and foodstuffs. At the same time, it had the main concentration of luxury industries and was the largest port. City of London merchants, apart from being wealthier than their provincial counterparts, controlled a large proportion of the country's commerce through their great trading concerns, such as the East India Company. London also developed quickly as a major centre of finance, banking, and insurance. This meant that by the end of the century it had become firmly established as the European commercial entrepôt, handling goods from all over the world. Apart from this, as the capital city and centre of government, London housed the royal court and Parliament, which made it a highly influential centre of political, social and commercial preferment. This made it attractive to those with ambitions from all social levels, and many others came to enjoy the urban amenities, educational facilities and the fashionable London 'season' (see page 140). As a result, by the end of the seventeenth century London was not just England's largest town, but had become the real centre of the national economy. This transformed England from being a collection of provincial and local markets into an integrated national and international market.

The first stage of this process was the need to supply London's growing population with foodstuffs (see page 54) and other necessities, such as textiles, ironmongery and coal. By the 1650s uniform national prices for textiles, coal, grain, cheese, cattle and hosiery had been established based on those in London.

## b) Improved Communications and Distribution

To achieve this more efficient distribution required improved transport by road, river and sea as commodities had to be brought in from ever increasing distances. Already in the early seventeenth century the Home Counties could no longer feed all of London. Grain - the 60,000 quarters needed in 1615 had risen to 200,000 quarters by the 1680s - cheese and other dairy products had to be brought in from the Midlands and the Thames Valley, and cattle were being driven in increasing numbers from the North for fattening. During the second half of the century considerable progress was made in making the Thames and other rivers, especially in the Midlands and the North, more navigable by building bridges to replace fords and by removing weirs and other obstructions. Roads were gradually made more passable at all times of the year, especially with the introduction of turnpike trusts after 1660.

These were created by groups of neighbouring businessmen and landowners to finance the repair and maintenance of the roads linking towns. At the same time, the provision of signposts and milestones helped travellers and facilitated the exchange of goods. Better river navigation and roads meant that larger barges, ferries, four-wheeled waggons (drawn by 12 horses and carrying 70 cwt of goods compared with the 20 cwt capacity of the old two-wheeled cart) and coaches could carry more produce and people over longer distances. Even by the 1630s regular weekly services by 2,000 registered carriers, conveying passengers, goods and letters by road and river, had been established to link London with all the larger provincial towns. Heavier goods were transported by sea, and the capital's need for coal and other materials stimulated east coast trade as fleets of colliers and coasters plied between Newcastle and London (see page 62). This in turn was helped by harbour improvements and increased shipbuilding for both coastal and oceanic trade.

Such measures were highly necessary because there had to be an increasingly sophisticated level of exchange between the capital and the provinces to replace and supplement the traditional markets and fairs. Apart from redistributing overseas imports, London offered an increasing number of specialist facilities and products ranging from banking, insurance and printing to clocks, silks, porcelain and jewellery. These were supplied to the provinces in return for foodstuffs, manufactures and raw materials from the countryside for resale and export. This necessitated a growing amount of travel as London merchants or their agents and provincial businessmen and landowners negotiated deals and arranged transportation, finance and credit. In this way London was exerting an increasing influence on the whole country and breaking down any residual localism. The provincial capitals and market towns modelled themselves on London by providing similar facilities on a smaller scale. The spread of shops even into the smallest towns meant that a much greater variety of goods was becoming available to all levels of society. This process was helped by growing numbers of newspapers which were distributed widely to carry news and advertising from the capital.

## c) The Development of Banking

These developments made it very important for a sound banking and financial structure to be established. The first stage in this process was the improvement in credit facilities and monetary exchange brought about by the growing use of bills of exchange. Dealing within the metropolitan market depended on credit. London and provincial merchants, dealers and their agents bought goods on credit from the suppliers through a bill of debt or a bill of exchange, signed by both parties, giving the date when payment was due. As the supplier was giving credit, and taking a risk that he might not be paid, he charged more than the actual value of goods, which represented a form of interest. In 1571 interest had been fixed at 10 per cent, but the rates fell steadily down to 5 per cent by 1713. If the buyer settled up before the due date he paid less than the full amount as a discount. Much the same principle was used in marine insurance and underwriting, with several people combining to share the risk. A ship and its cargo were insured for their value and an additional sum added to cover loss. The premium was calculated on the amount of risk involved, which depended on the destination of the ship and whether the country was at war. By the 1660s London had acquired considerable skill in this type of credit transfer, and bills drawn on London were cheaper than those on the continent. They were recognised all over the world. It was this that helped London to become the major European entrepôt. English commercial and financial expertise had surpassed that of the Dutch, who had previously dominated in this area. By the eighteenth century London brokers and underwriters meeting in the coffee houses, particularly Lloyds, largely controlled this side of world commerce and earned England valuable income through the invisible earnings of marine insurance.

Apart from its commercial importance, the bond of exchange became the basis for the early forms of banking. Bills could be used by creditors to pay off their debts to third parties, and so became a form of currency. Provincial landowners and businessmen coming to London could draw on their credit to supply them with funds during their visit. Similarly. those with credit in London and in their local town could transfer money between the two. Soon goldsmiths, merchants and other businessmen in London and the larger provincial towns were allowing customers to make payments and withdrawals from their current accounts, and, for a fee, to run up overdrafts. The next stage was for these bankers to issue bank notes, give loans and overdrafts, run current and deposit accounts, deal in stocks and shares, and provide insurance. In London two forms of bank emerged. Those in the East End dealt mainly in commercial matters, while those in the West End catered mainly for the private customer. The London and provincial banks generally co-operated well, providing a flexible national financial structure, much to the advantage of commercial development within the domestic market.

The final stage in the process came in the 1690s when the government was having great difficulty in raising loans to finance the war with France. A major reason for this was that after the Civil War the growing demand for freedom of individual trading and the ending of monopolies had weakened the power of the wealthy City merchant dynasties in favour of rising financiers and entrepreneurs. As a result the old trading monopolies, such as the Russia and Levant Companies, and even temporarily the East India Company (see page 84), were in difficulties, and could no longer supply sufficient loans to the government. In 1694 a consortium of bankers raised a loan of

£1,200,000 and was given a temporary charter for four years allowing them to issue shares as the Bank of England, with the loan secured against taxes and customs duties. This proved a popular investment with the royal court, city interests and landowners. As the French wars continued and became even more expensive the charter was extended, and by 1715 the Bank of England had become a permanent institution with a capital of £10 million. Apart from being the sole lender to the government, it was joint stock limited liability bank. As such it could issue bank notes, deal in bullion, allow transfers by cheques and give overdrafts to large companies and other banks. The creation of a national bank was the final stage in the process of making London the major financial centre in world trade. At the same time it placed the now fully integrated metropolitan market on a firm footing for future expansion.

## 7 Conclusion: Economic Growth in the Stuart Economy

The lack of reliable statics for both the domestic and overseas markets makes it impossible to measure the actual amount of economic growth during the seventeenth century. For similar reasons the real degree of expansion in the agricultural and industrial sectors is equally uncertain. What is clear is that a considerable structural change had taken place within the economy. The domestic market had become much more sophisticated than it had been in 1600. The transfer of labour from agriculture into the manufacturing and services industries was taking place much more efficiently. Communications by land, sea and inland water were improved rapidly, and a secure financial and banking system had been put in place. Abroad England had established herself as a major naval and commercial power. Enforcement of the Navigation Acts meant that England had a secure supply of cheap raw materials and an expanding colonial market for domestic exports. Although the Dutch continued to dominate trade with the East Indies, the East India Company had become firmly established in India. Furthermore, England had gained control of the highly lucrative, 'triangular' slave trade, and dominated the re-export and carrying trades. London had emerged as the leading European city, and had become the entrepôt for world trade. This was a considerable economic achievement. Although England's commercial position was to be challenged, particularly by the French, during the eighteenth century, a very secure foundation for continued expansion had been laid by the time of the signing of the Treaty of Utrecht in 1713.

There had been a remarkable growth in England's share of world commerce betweeen 1660 and 1700, but this should not be allowed to overshadow the importance of the domestic economy. It is considered that improved agricultural performance was highly significant. Not only did the agricultural sector produce sufficient food and industrial raw materials for domestic needs, but it did so with a smaller workforce, so releasing labour for industry. At the same time, much of the investment in both industry and commerce came from wealth generated through agriculture. Industrial developments, especially in the craft trades, was also highly important for sustained growth. Although much of the commercial expansion up to 1700 had been based on importing and re-exporting colonial raw materials and other foreign goods, during the eighteenth century the major advance was in the export of domestic manufactures. In any case, much of the success of the Stuart economy was based on rising demand in the home market, rather than overseas expansion. Greater spending power had been made possible by the demographic changes that had brought rising living standards to all but the lowest sections of society. Previously the major area of demand had come from the landed and urban elites, and this had been mainly for imported luxury goods. The expansion of the middle orders and their emulation of the elites (see page 116) greatly enlarged the amount demand for both luxury and consumer items. Even among the lower orders there is evidence of greater spending on cheap consumer goods from chapmen, carriers and small back street shops. It was the creation of a mass consumer market, based on higher living standards and rising social and economic aspirations, that was probably the major contributor to economic growth by the early eighteenth century.

---

*Making notes on* '*The Economy: Overseas Trade, London and the Metropolitan Market*'

The first section looks at some of theories of world trade (you should also refer back to your notes on chapter 1) and at contemporary attitudes towards commerce and economic growth. You should compare these ideas and decide how they help to explain commmercial expansion in the second half of the seventeenth century. Section 2 examines the problems facing late Tudor and early Stuart commerce. Note carefully the various difficulties and decide what were the main causes of the trade depression up to the 1650s. Section 3 examines how the foundations of English commercial interests were laid in the Americas, the Caribbean and the Far East. Note carefully the main types of trade being developed in each area. The next section examines how England established herself as a major commercial power after 1650. Make careful notes and decide to what extent the Navigation Acts, naval power and an aggressive foreign policy helped to expand English trade. Section 5 explores the development of English commerce after 1660. Careful consideration needs to given to how successfully colonial, Eastern and European commerce linked together, and the importance of the re-export trade. Section 6 examines the emergence of London as the centre of world and the development of an integrated national market. You need to make careful notes on the developments and compare the importance of the domestic market with demand created through world trade. Finally look back at your notes on chapter 3 to decide why and to what extent the Stuart economy had expanded after the 1650s.

## Answering essay questions on the Stuart Economy

When preparing yourself to answer questions on the Stuart Economy it is sensible to focus your attention on the three relatively distinct aspects of agriculture, industry and trade (subdivided into 'overseas' and

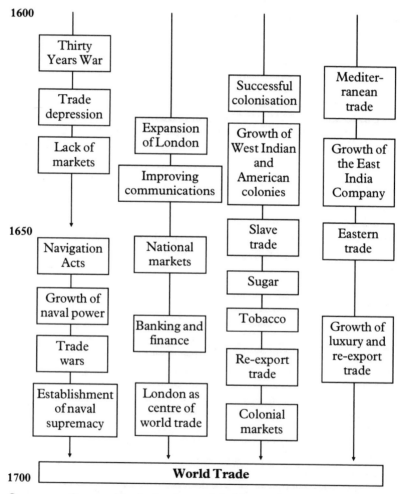

*Summary - Overseas Trade, London and the Metropolitan Market*

'internal'). It would also be worthwhile being ready to write about 'London' as a separate topic. Of all the approaches you could adopt in undertaking this work, exploring the concept of 'change and continuity' could prove to be the most productive. Examine the following questions and decide why this is so.

1 Do you agree that 'English agriculture changed dramatically between 1600 and 1700'?
2 Was there an industrial revolution in seventeenth-century England?
3 Why did the pattern of English overseas trade alter so much during the Stuart period?
4 What effect did the growth of London during the seventeenth century have on the English economy as a whole?
5 How far was the growth of the English economy between 1660 and 1714 the result of improvements in the country's infrastructure?
6 What were the major causes of change in the seventeenth-century English economy?

All of these questions are relatively straightforward as long as the usual processes of question analysis are gone through. Each has one or two easily identifiable key phrases to be thought about, and there are few hidden snags. Question 3 has one of the complications that is frequently found with 'why?' questions - the need to 'unpack' the 'what?' that the 'why?' is being asked about. (You might find it helpful to explain the previous sentence to yourself in explicit terms.) Question 6 poses the normal problem implicit in seemingly simple questions - how to avoid giving a low-level answer. However, it is not difficult to discover the way out of the problem. What is it?

---

***Source-based questions on*** *'The Economy: Overseas Trade, London and the Metropolitan Market'*

**1 The Navigation Act (1660) and its Possible Effects**
Carefully read the extracts on pages 76 and 77. Answer the following questions.
a) Using evidence from both extracts, explain the aims of the Navigation Act. (5 marks)
b) In what ways does the Navigation Act reflect mercantilist ideas? (4 marks)
c) What were the worries of the colonists as reflected in the second extract? (4 marks)
d) To what extent and for what reasons did the fears of the colonists prove to be groundless? (5 marks)
e) Why was it that the petition from which the second extract is taken was presented to Parliament by a London merchant? (2 marks)

# CHAPTER 5

# Society: The Landed Elites, the Pseudo-Gentry and the Middle Orders

## 1 Introduction: Definitions, Issues and Approaches

Since the mid 1950s there has been a fierce debate over the course and nature of social change in Stuart society (see chapter 1). Clearly there is an enormous gulf between Marxist perceptions of a society becoming increasingly polarised along the lines of mutually antagonistic classes and some revisionist visions of a society which remained a virtually unchanged, land-based hierarchy of status until the mid-nineteenth century. The reality lies somewhere between these two extremes. Change was taking place, but as part of a long-term evolutionary process, rather than as a dramatic, revolutionary transformation. During the Stuart period the process of social change appears to have quickened, but society itself became more stable after 1660. Although there is no consensus to explain this apparent paradox, it is possible to identify some of the major trends and issues within society in general which will be discussed in detail below and in chapters 6 and 7.

### a) The Landed Elites

One of the central themes of debate has been the 'rise of the gentry' (see page 2). In broad terms by 1600 the numbers of the gentry had exceeded the available supply of land, even allowing for the extensive sale of monastic and Crown estates from the 1540s. This is seen as marking the end of general expansion of the landed gentry. At the same time the growth in the numbers and wealth of the gentry had created a great demand for new titles to mark their improved status. Tudor monarchs had been careful not to create too many new titles, but the Stuarts, in contrast, were very liberal in this respect. This meant that, in addition to a shrinking land market, there was an 'inflation of honours' among the aristocracy and greater gentry who were seeking more land to support their new status (see page 103). At the same time during the seventeenth century many of the 'mere' or lesser gentry were having to sell up through being unable to meet the high costs of improving their estates (see page 53). This process became particularly marked after the 1660s because many of the gentry who had fought in the Civil War had become impoverished and their estates had been ruined during the conflict. This led to a process of consolidation whereby the aristocracy and greater gentry enlarged their holdings by acquiring property previously held by the lesser gentry. By the end of the seventeenth century the land market had become very restricted making it difficult for younger sons of elite families or new entrants to obtain estates. This is seen as the major cause of the growth of what has been called the pseudo-gentry. The Stuart elites continued to marry young and produce large families which meant that there were numerous younger sons in search of estates and careers. Increasingly they were going to London and other towns to enter trade or the professions. Many were successful but had no opportunity to buy a country estate. Alongside them were the many successful lawyers, civil servants, financiers and merchants who previously would have expected eventually to enter the landed gentry through purchasing land. Their wealth enabled many of this group to lead the leisured lifestyle of the landed elites and live in town dwellings that mirrored the opulence of fashionable country houses. For this reason they have become known as the landless gentry or pseudo-gentry.

## b) The Pseudo-Gentry

The pseudo-gentry formed part of the section of society loosely defined by modern historians as the middle orders. Lawrence Stone in his article *Social Mobility in England 1500-1700* (1966), identified the four top groups in this category as merchants, lawyers, administrators and the clergy. To these could be added a range of professionals in the sciences, medicine, music, surveying, architecture, the visual arts or landscape gardening. These people were not part of the traditional rural social structure which consisted of the landed elites and the vast mass of the lower orders who gained their living mainly from the land.

For this reason contemporary writers in the sixteenth and early seventeenth centuries found it very difficult, apart from the merchants, to fit them into their perception of the social order (see page 98). It was not until the end of the seventeenth century that commentators such as Gregory King in the *Estimate of the Comparative Strength of Great Britain* (1696) (see page 106) began to classify such people with any confidence. King calculated that in 1688 there were 65,000 people in these categories, which meant that they and their families (372,520) amounted to about 7 per cent of his estimated population of 5,500,520. This fits quite well with modern estimations that these groups, along with the landed elites, (which according to King's figures amounted to 3 per cent) comprised between 10 and 15 per cent of the population by 1700.

During the seventeenth century most of the people within these groups prospered because of the expansion in trade, increase in litigation, growth in the bureaucracy, and greater interest in medicine and the sciences. Even the higher and lower clergy, who had lost considerable status in the period following the Reformation, are thought to have regained much of their social position by the 1630s. By then they were better educated and were being recruited more from gentry and professional families. This was an important consideration that distinguished all these groups from the remainder of non-elite society. Many of them were the younger sons of the gentry, others were the direct descendants of elite families, and many were connected by marriage to both the gentry and the aristocracy. This is thought to be a major reason why by the end the seventeenth century trade was no longer looked upon as such a serious impediment to gaining genteel status. By that time many within this group were taking the titles of gentleman and esquire, or were being given the courtesy title of 'Mr' to mark their improved status. Indeed, an increasing number of landed families lived for part of the year in towns and engaged in some form of trade or profession.

## c) The Lesser Middle Orders

Their greater wealth and connection with the landed elites distinguished the pseudo-gentry from what can be called the lesser middle orders. The majority of this section of society came from the self-employed freemen and leaseholders in both town and countryside, consisting of yeomen, prosperous husbandmen, industrialists, craftsmen and shopkeepers. However, because many of these people followed more than one trade it is difficult to define them precisely. During the seventeenth century these more traditional occupations were augmented by an increasing number of inn keepers, minor officials and civil servants, clerks, dockyard officials, and agents employed in expanding country estates, banks and commerce. Judging by Gregory King's estimations, by 1688 some 39 per cent of the population formed part of this very fluid and mobile portion of society. Apart from the expansion in numbers there were several significant structural changes taking place within this group. One of the features of the sixteenth century had been the 'rise' of the yeomen (see page 8) but, like the 'mere' gentry, this group seems to have ceased to expand during the Stuart period. As early as 1600 Thomas Wilson in *The State of England*, was already commenting that 'the yeomanry of England is decayed'. He attributed this decline to growing commercial competition from the gentry. Certainly it seems that although many successful yeomen had managed to enter the ranks of the gentry by 1600 it became increasingly difficult thereafter. It has been suggested that this was because yeomen, unlike the urban elites, had less connection with the gentry through younger sons and marriage. At the same time many yeomen found the economic conditions after the Restoration (see page 53) difficult and were forced to sell up, or become leasehold farmers on the expanding estates of the greater gentry and aristocracy. The same is true for many of the prosperous husbandmen who, by the end of the seventeenth century, were having to change their copyhold tenure, which normally lasted for 21 years, for shorter and less secure leases. This was all part of the trend in commercial agriculture for there to be fewer but larger farms. Yeomen and husbandmen had always supplemented their farming incomes by having other occupations in the 'dual' economy (see page 119). After the 1660s they, and their children, were increasingly having to find full-time occupations in industry and the expanding service areas.

## d) Social Attitudes and Cultural Change

Stuart period social attitudes were changing not just towards the labouring poor but about society in general. Among the elites and the middle orders there was a growing confidence in man's ability to master and understand nature and the universe through the natural sciences. This can be seen as part of the growing rationality and optimism arising out of Renaissance and humanistic culture that was to develop in the Enlightenment of the eighteenth century. After the Restoration society is seen to have become polarised, with growing gaps opening up within and between social groups. To what extent this was a direct result of the Civil War is a matter of considerable debate (see page 149). To a certain extent these cultural developments seem to be mainly the result of natural evolution rather than any marked shift in ideology. However, it is likely that reaction to the horrors of warfare, and against the austerity of the Protectorate, did have some effect. By the early eighteenth century the two major rifts within society were those between the rich and the poor and between men and women. The landed and urban elites and the middling orders were becoming increasingly richer, while the labouring masses, despite some improvement in living standards were still struggling to subsist. It appears that this gap was made even more noticeable by growing educational and cultural differences, especially after 1660. Education, which had been available largely to all levels of society between 1540 and 1640, became much more restricted after the Restoration (see page 102).

This affected two sections of society in particular - women and the labouring poor. The illiterate labouring poor are considered to have continued their irrational belief in traditional oral popular culture. This is seen as distancing them still further from the remainder of society which was becoming increasingly literate and rational (see page 149). There is still considerable debate over this issue and the whole question of literacy in general. Certainly the lack of educational opportunities is claimed to have added to the sexual polarisation between men and women at all levels of society. Women are considered to have become more 'marginalised'. Amongst the elites marriage was seen as the only career for women, and wives were expected to enhance their husbands' status, to be submissive and to bear male children. Middle-order wives were being increasingly prevented from sharing in their husband's occupations, because their enforced leisure was supposed to enhance the family's social status. A growing sexual division of labour is considered to have been developing in the labour market, with the 'frailty' of women being made an excuse to make many of the best paid jobs male dominated (see page 120).

After 1660 the emphasis on private property and the growth of leisure also helped to accentuate the gulf between rich and poor. In part the growing importance attached to private property may be seen as a direct result of the abolition of feudal taxation and the Court of Wards (see page 15). This meant that the Crown no longer had the right to tax or take over the management of landed estates if the heir was under age. At the same time the acceptance of the enclosure of agricultural land eroded communal rights and access to the commons for the labouring poor (see page 125). Property rights were increasingly enshrined in the law, and trespass and poaching became capital offences. Similarly, many traditional rights and perquisites such as gleaning, wool gathering, or workmen keeping the waste off-cuts of their trade became regarded as theft.

The return of Charles II in 1660 was greeted with widespread rejoicing, which is considered to have been a reaction to the lack-lustre austerity of the Protectorate. The Restoration period is seen as one of increasing leisure and pleasure for the elites. Such a lifestyle was seen as the hallmark of status among the middling orders who were trying to emulate their social superiors. While moralists criticised the growing promiscuity and sexual licence among the elites, they were even more condemnatory of the supposed preference for drink and leisure among the labouring poor (see chapters 6 and 7).

## 2 Changes in the Elite and Middle-Order Social Structure

Many social historians and contemporary commentators see the structure of this part of society becoming more complicated by the late seventeenth century. What is more difficult is to identify the nature of the change that was taking place. Sir Thomas Smith and William Harrison when describing the late Tudor society in which they lived both divided it into four groups. At the top was the peerage of barons, viscounts, earls, marquesses and dukes. Next came the knights, esquires and gentlemen of the gentry. The third category consisted of burgesses of the towns and 40-shilling freeholders in the countryside. The remainder of the population formed the fourth estate and consisted of all those who did not have freehold land or who worked for wages. In 1600 John Hooker when describing the people of Devon defined the social structure very simply. He wrote that there were four sorts and degrees of people: 'noblemen and gentlemen, the merchant, the yeoman and the labourer'. This view is largely true of all the commentators of the late sixteenth and early seventeenth centuries. Although there was some discussion about where merchants, the clergy or the rising profession of lawyers fitted into the structure, it seems that it was commonly felt that society was a divinely appointed and unchanging hierarchy based on traditional values.

## a) The Influence of Religion and the Civil War

It is very clear that not all people thought of society in the early seventeenth century along these lines. The debate among historians about the impact of Protestantism and Puritanism on social ideas is still far from resolved (see page 14). It is not easy to determine whether the Puritans and other religious, sectarian reformers were just a very vocal and unpopular minority, or whether they had a deep and lasting impact on social thinking. During the 1640s the Levellers, who are seen as the most democratic of the Puritan groups, did attempt to bring in social reform, but only in a very limited form. Their demands for the extension of the franchise envisaged greater rights only for property holders and the self-employed, and specifically excluded the wage earners and the poor. The really radical demands came from the True Levellers, (see page 5), who wished to see the abolition of private property and total equality for all men and some even for women. However, their ideas seem to have gained very little support even among the labouring poor. Certainly, the elites, both Puritan and royalist, closed ranks against these threats from below, and during the Protectorate no fundamental attempt was made to alter the social structure.

## b) The Impact of the 'Educational Revolution'

Although in many respects the impact of Puritans and Protestantism upon the structure of society is open to question, in terms of education they appear to have had a considerable influence. Between 1540 and 1640 there was what has been termed an 'educational revolution'. The English Reformation of the 1530s and 1540s ended the clergy's monopoly over education and opened up educational opportunities for the whole of the laity. In particular this is seen as benefiting the professional and middling orders of society which were expanding in numbers and wealth. They saw the greater educational opportunities in secondary and higher education as ideal vocational training to improve the career prospects of their children. This, along with the greater numbers of the landed elites and even the poorer sections of society gaining more education, is considered to have led to an enormous increase in literacy and training by 1640. The growth of educational opportunities is thought to have quickened the pace of structural change by helping to expand the middle ranks of society. At the same time it is considered to have led to the growing debate about religion and politics and about the place of women in society that took place in the first half of the seventeenth century.

## c) The Place of Women in Society

During the seventeenth century the standing of women within society is seen to have deteriorated, and this promoted a fierce debate among male and female writers. By the late sixteenth century, partly through the influence and example of Elizabeth I, women's place in society and their right to be educated is considered to have improved. However, after Elizabeth's death there was a male reaction against the freedom of women and an attempt to reinforce all the old sexual double standards and stereotypes. Because of the original sin of Eve all women were regarded as weak and open to temptation, and there was even discussion about whether women had souls. Women's passions were seen as too strong for their weak intellects, and this, allied to their supposed sexual insatiability, was thought to encourage them into carnal promiscuity. It was argued not only that they were physically weaker than men but that their brains were different, making them intellectually inferior and virtually incapable of being educated. These points were constantly being hammered home by male writers such as Joseph Swetnam in *The Arraignment of Lewd, Idle, Forward and Unconstant Women* published in 1615. At the same time females were portrayed as the softer, gentler sex in need of male guidance. The proper place for women was seen as being married, looking after the home and the children, and being meek and submissive to their husbands.

This picture was not universally accepted and there was a lively exchange of views between both male and female contributors. Books, such as Richard Braithwaite's *The English Gentlewoman* of 1531, praising the timid, modest and virtuous woman as being a 'crown' to her husband, were countered by works like the anonymous Mary Tittle-well and Joan Hit-him-hard's *The Women's Sharpe Revenge* of 1640 which attacked such stereotyping. Woman continued to assert their independence during the Civil War. Elite wives, such as Mary Lady Bankes who defended Corfe castle for two years, for the royalists and Brilliana Lady Harley who held Brampton Bryan castle for the Parliamentarians, won respect from both sides. Women from all ranks were involved in the war helping and fighting in the many sieges of towns and houses, while some donned male attire and fought in the infantry and cavalry. Others became involved in political debates of the 1640s and in representations to Parliament. In a *Petition of Women* to Parliament in 1648 it was commented 'that since we are assured of our creation in the image of God ... we cannot but wonder and grieve that we should appear so despicable in your eyes as to be thought unworthy to petition or represent our grievances to this honourable House ... Would you keep us at home in our houses ...?' Certainly it appears that during the disruption caused by the Civil War some women seized the opportunity to take a more independent role and to escape from male domination. However, many historians consider that such small numbers of women were actively involved, either in the war or the literary debate, that they are untypical, and that most Stuart women accepted their subordinate place within the structure of society (see page 109).

## d) The Influence of the Protectorate

Under the military rule of the Protectorate the debate over changes to the social structure and the independence of women came to an end. The Church of England was swept away and with it, to some extent, went traditional views of society. The Puritan ideal of the righteous rule of 'God's elect' was superimposed on the old accepted authority of the landed elites. An attempt was made to reform the manners of all social ranks and to turn England into a 'godley' society. Extravagance, lavish dress, drunkenness, gambling, gaming and theatres were condemned and were suppressed as far as possible. Christmas, Easter and Whitsun were turned into fast days, and the sabbath was strictly enforced on Sundays. At the same time there were proposals for educational reforms. The curriculum was to become more scientific and less classically orientated, there was to be universal elementary education, and a new university was to be founded at Durham. It was thought that more schooling would be a way of establishing social and political obedience among the unruly masses.

## e) The 'Restoration' of Society?

The accession of Charles II restored the 'old order'. The return of the Church of England brought with it, seemingly, the traditional concepts of a divinely appointed, hierarchical society of status. Yet it is apparent that it was recognised by the restored monarch and his advisers that significant and unwelcome social change had occurred among the middling and lower ranks of society. Education was blamed as a root

---

The Duke of Newcastle, Advice to Charles II, 1660

1 After the Reformation and the Dissolution of the abbeys, then the law crept up, and at last grew to be so numerous and to such a vast body as it swelled to be too big for the kingdom, and hath been no small means to foment and continue this late and unfortunate
5 rebellion. How to diminish them would be a hard work; they have taken so deep a root in England. To lessen their fees will not do it. Fewer grammar schools would do well, for if you cut off too much reading and writing, there must be fewer lawyers and consequently clerks, ... The Bible under every weaver's and chambermaid's arms
10 hath done us much hurt. That which made it one way is the universities. Abounds with too many scholars. Therefore, if every

college had but half the number, they would be better fed and as
well taught. But that which hath done most hurt is the abundance
of grammar schools and inns of courts. The Treasurer Burghley
15 said there were too many grammar schools, because it made the
plough and the cart to be neglected, which was to feed and defend
us, for there are very few that can read that will put their hands to
the plough or the cart ... and there are very few that can read will
carry a musket. And there are so many schools now as most read.
20 So indeed there should be, but such a proportion as to serve the
church and moderately the law and the merchants, and the rest for
labour, for else they run out to idle and unnecessary people that
becomes a factious burthern to the Commonwealth. For when
most was unlettered, it was much a better world for both peace and
25 war.

---

cause of social disharmony by creating too many literate people for the
economic needs of the country. In the atmosphere of ultra-conservatism
after 1660 education became unfashionable.

## f) The End of the Educational Revolution

The effect of this is considered to have accentuated the cultural divisions
within the structure of society. Certainly the numbers of those attending
and matriculating from the universities declined after the 1660s. The
landed elites appear to have continued to use the grammar schools and
then the universities and Inns of Court more as finishing schools to give
them an acceptable cultural background in the classics and the law.
Women from all ranks of society were virtually excluded from
education. A basic ability to read and write in English, and then training
in the necessary skills to become a good wife and mother was all that was
thought necessary for elite and middle-order daughters. For the sons
and daughters of the lower orders, instruction in useful economic
activities to prepare them for work became the norm. The numbers
entering education in some form from the professional middling ranks
also appears to have declined. However, the Act of Uniformity of 1660
and the Test Act of 1673 excluded Nonconformists from grammar
schools, universities and Inns of Court and from all public office. For
this reason many went to their own schools and dissenting academies.
These changes are considered to have brought about a general decline in
educational standards which lasted until the early twentieth century.

## g) Landed and Polite Society

Although there was a very conservative outlook after 1660 this did not mean that the social structure did not continue to evolve. The peerage and the landed elites became more exclusive because the limited land market made it more difficult for potential new entrants to their class to acquire estates. These groups held most of the landed property and a high proportion of the wealth. It was no longer easy for younger sons of the wealthy sections of the middle orders to ensure their status by purchasing land. Herein lay the greater stability of late Stuart society in comparison with the fluid situation created by the hectic Tudor land market and the rapid inflation of honours up to 1640. Increasing numbers who followed the lifestyle of the elites had to remain as the landless pseudo-gentry of the towns. Certainly it appears that by the early eighteenth century participation in and connections with the professions, commerce, banking and industry no longer carried the social stigma that they had a century earlier. Land was being seen more as a commodity to be exploited to create wealth, rather than just a source of rents and status. However, it does not appear that wealth was seen as a complete substitute for land and birth. The peerage and the squirearchy still regarded themselves as the backbone of society and expected to be treated with the deference that went with their position, even if they themselves engaged in the professions, finance, commerce and industry.

## h) Changes in the Middling Orders

While the landed elites can be seen to have been more stable, the amount of change within the middling ranks of society was increasing. These groups were expanding in both numbers and wealth. In addition to natural growth from large middle-order families, there was a constant stream of new recruits from the children of the landed elites. At the same time the greater economic opportunities in industry and services led to some upward mobility from the lower orders. The improved economic conditions after the 1660s aided this process, and added to the wealth of the middle orders. Denied the opportunity to improve their status by acquiring land, the rich increasingly adopted the culture and leisured lifestyle of the landed elites.

They, in turn, were copied by those just below them in terms of wealth - a process of emulation which went down the social scale. This is seen as boosting demand and fostering the expanding leisure industries and so creating a consumer society. It is also considered to have promoted cultural differentiation. Even those at the very bottom the middling ranks wished to distinguish themselves from the labouring poor and to be considered as part of polite and respectable society.

## 3 Social Change and Mobility

The main methods of social mobility for the landed elites and the middling orders through inheritance, marriage and acquiring wealth remained the same throughout the period. After 1660 the increasingly static land market made it more difficult, but by no means impossible, for the non-elites to acquire estates, but wealth and lifestyle were also becoming to be regarded as an important mark of status. In any case, although land was an important source of wealth, fortunes could be made more quickly from commerce, finance, the colonies and the professions. This makes it difficult to be very precise about the relative success of any particular group, because individual fortune was so varied. Ownership of an estate could depend on a fortunate marriage, or a disastrous night's gambling. A younger brother might make a fortune with the East India Company, while his elder brother lived in poverty on the family estate. A daughter might marry a duke, elope with an impecunious curate, become a famous actress, or live in genteel poverty as an unmarried companion or governess. By the late seventeenth century there were more means of advancement through the expansion of the professions, the arts, central and local government, commerce, banking and finance, industry, the colonies, the navy and the army. Equally, downward mobility, debt and destitution through misfortune, speculation, gambling or drink was just as likely.

## a) The 'Inflation of Honours'

One of the features of the early seventeenth century was the 'inflation of honours' among the landed elites. In 1603 it is estimated that there were 61 nobles, 350 knights, and about 2,000 esquires and 15,000 gentlemen. This was a mark of the unwillingness of the Tudors, and especially Elizabeth I, to confer titles at a time when the landed elites were expanding rapidly. Although the numbers of esquires and gentlemen possibly trebled during the sixteenth century, the total of nobles had remained constant and there were probably fewer knights. This situation created a demand for titles to go with land and wealth, which James I was very willing to supply. He created more than 900 knights during the first 4 months of his reign. Anyone with an income of over £40 a year was allowed to apply for a knighthood, and the honour was freely sold by the king, his friends and courtiers. This had the effect of devaluing the title and during the course of the century the numbers fell, so that by 1688 Gregory King estimated that there were only 600 knights.

Such a flood of new creations annoyed many of the older and wealthier greater gentry families who required some means to distinguish themselves from the remainder of the gentry. In 1611 the new hereditary title of baronet was created. At first this was to be limited to 200 people; applicants had to have land worth over £1,000 a year, and be able to prove that their family had had a coat of arms for at least three generations. The new title could be purchased for £1,095 payable to the Exchequer in three instalments. However, James and his favourites were chronically short of money and baronetcies were soon being sold to rich London merchants and others for lump-sum down payments. Once again this led to the devaluing of the title and by 1622 the asking price had fallen to £220. Even in the 1640s there were some 400 baronets and by 1688 the number had risen to 800.

A similar process was taking place with the distribution of noble titles. Until 1615 the creation and promotion of noble families remained quite respectable, with only families who had risen to prominence under the Tudors, such as the Cecils and the Spencers, receiving new titles. Then through the influence of the new favourite, the Duke of Buckingham, there was a rapid sale of titles. This brought 'new' men such as the Earl of Craven, a former lord mayor of London, into the peerage. In 1615 the nobility had increased to only 80, but by 1628 it had expanded to over 120. The original asking price for a barony, the promotion of a baron to an earl, or the creation of a viscount was about £10,000. However, these prices fell to about £4,000 by the late 1620s. Charles I was more cautious in his creations, and in the 1640s the peerage still totalled about 120. By 1688 the new creations of the Restoration had increased the peerage to about 160, but thereafter the numbers remained fairly constant.

## b) Land Ownership

The effect of this expansion of titles in itself put more strain on a land market already under pressure from the growth in the numerical strength of the elites. It was this situation, with the added stresses caused by the Civil War and the more stringent economic conditions after 1660, that led to many smaller gentry estates being amalgamated into those of their wealthier neighbours. However, this caused only a slight shift in the balance of land ownership in overall terms. Following the closure of the monasteries in 1540 there had been a marked movement of land away from the Crown and the Church. Before the English Reformation about 35 per cent of land had been held by the king or the regular and secular clergy, but by 1700 this had fallen to about 10 per cent. The nobility's share of land remained relatively constant over the period at about 20 per cent. The level may have fallen slightly by the early seventeenth century, but recovered after 1660. The major beneficiaries of the redistribution had been the gentry and yeomen, who still held some 45 and 25 per cent of land respectively by the early eighteenth century.

## c) Wealth and Income

In terms of wealth there was little change in the relative position between the landed elites during the period. However, it must be remembered that, because of fragmentary evidence, annual variations, and the problem of deciding what forms of income should be used, it is very difficult to make any really accurate estimate of average income. In 1688 King calculated that peers had an average income of £2,800 a year, baronets £880, knights £650, esquires £450 and gentlemen £280. Although his estimates are considered to be slightly low, King's figures correspond very well with most modern and contemporary calculations for various periods in respect of the difference in income between the groups. It appears that the average income for peers was 70 per cent higher than the average for baronets, while the difference between baronets, knights, esquires and gentlemen was about 30 per cent. Although an interesting statistic, it conceals the considerable variations within and between the groups. A duke with estates amounting to tens of thousands of acres and an income of £50,000 a year is far removed from a country gentleman with an estate of 200 acres and an income of £90 a year. Yet, on the other hand, while many gentry families had annual incomes of up to £20,000, some barons only had £200 or £300 a year. In any case, to put the position in perspective, some London merchants and lawyers had fortunes well in excess of £100,000.

Similarly wide variations existed in the incomes of the middle orders. However, King's estimates do give a generally accurate picture of the pattern of incomes by the end of the seventeenth century. The average income of the 26 (actually 27) archbishops and bishops was estimated at £1,300 a year, which places them well above the gentry in economic terms. Otherwise, overseas merchants had the highest average income of £400, and were estimated to earn twice as much as internal traders. The next highest income group were senior civil servants with an average annual income of £240, while lawyers averaged £140 a year. The remainder of the middle-order annual incomes was estimated to range from £84 for yeomen and some freeholders down to £40 for skilled workers. Careers as officers in the army and navy appear to have been quite a good prospect with incomes of £80 and £60 a year respectively. In contrast, for most people a career in the Church still did not seem very inviting with the stipends of the lower clergy averaging only £45 a year.

## d) Change and Social Mobility in the County Community

Another way of assessing the amount of social change during the Stuart period is to examine the county communities. After 1660 elite and middling society in the provinces is considered to have become much more conservative and stable, even in radical counties like Suffolk and Northamptonshire, which had been prominently Parliamentarian in the Civil War. This is seen as part of the stabilisation of the land market and reaction to the war. However, there were still wide variations between county communities. Some were dominated by a noble family, such as the Percys in Northumberland, or by one two greater gentry families, while in others there were no leading families.

North-west Berkshire is typical of what was happening in many counties. By 1600 there were 44 resident gentry families of whom 16 had been there since the 1520s. Another 16 were of non-landed elite origins; 2 courtiers, 3 yeomen, 3 former tenants, 5 London merchants, 2 local clothiers and a lawyer. By 1640 the number of resident gentry families had risen to 49, including 13 of the original families from 1520. There were 4 new entrants; 2 London merchants, the wealthy Pratt family, and a London lawyer rich enough to buy up 5 manors and to lend £3,000 to Charles I. In 1665 there were only 37 resident gentry families and no new entrants. Only 4 of the families from the 1520s remained, but 20 of the others had been there since the 1550s. Several families had to sell all or some of their estates, but apart from those acquired by the Earl of Craven, these had been bought by their neighbours.

None of the four leading gentry families in the 1520s were still there in the 1660s. The Fettiplaces and the Hydes had sold most of their land and moved to neighbouring counties. The Essex family had gone bankrupt in the early seventeenth century, and the Norreys had become Earls of Banbury. The Yates, who had been merchants in 1520, had risen to the rank of baronet, despite being Catholics. The Southbys had been yeomen in the 1520s but had acquired several manors by the 1660s and had reached the status of esquires. The two oldest families, the Eystons and Puseys were still resident and were content to remain in their role as parish gentry. Among the newer families there were two baronets, three knights, seven esquires. The remainder were still just gentlemen.

Apart from the resident landed gentry the heralds listed another 16 esquires and 25 gentlemen when they visited north-west Berkshire in 1665 to decide which families were of genteel status. A number of these were younger children of the landed gentry, some were freeholders and others were tradesmen in the local towns. Francis Hyde is recorded as being a bootmaker in Reading, but as the eleventh son of Edward Hyde esquire, late of Denchworth, he was entitled to call himself a gentleman. The Aldworths who had been tanners and yeomen in the town of Wantage since the beginning the sixteenth century were now styled as gentlemen. The characteristic of all this group was that they had little or no land and can be seen as an excellent example of the pseudo-gentry. This was happening in other counties and towns all over the country. Many freeholders and tradesmen in both town and country were beginning to style themselves as gentlemen or esquires. At the same time a growing number of the landed gentry were buying town houses in order to enjoy the fashionable 'season', to engage in a trade or a profession, or to enable them to vote in borough elections.

## e) The Clergy

The social position of the clergy is not easy to assess. Certainly their social esteem had risen since the Elizabethan period. The main reason for this was that they were better educated - by 1640 the majority of parish clergy had degrees. However, the disestablishment of the Church of England under the Commonwealth further weakened the authority of the clergy. This process was continued after 1660 by the declining influence of religion throughout society, and the growth of dissenting churches outside the restored Church of England. In addition, many of the stipends remained low, even after the introduction of Queen Anne's Bounty which used some royal revenue from the Church to supplement poorer parishes. Yet, it appears that younger sons of the gentry and professional groups were entering the late Stuart Church in greater numbers.

After 1688 the higher clergy were really little more than political appointees of the Whig and Tory parties. In the parishes there was still considerable absenteeism and pluralism to compensate for lack of income. Even so, there were many well connected and wealthy rectors. At the same time the gentry often used vacancies in their local church to appoint one of their younger sons or a nephew to the living. This meant that the clergy were very much of the same status as the gentry. The close link between the squire and the 'hunting, shooting and fishing' parson of the eighteenth century was beginning to be established.

## f) Social Mobility and Status

The diversity and mobility among the elites and the middle orders steadily increased during the seventeenth century, producing an almost indefinable social mix. This section of society can be loosely separated into three groups, membership of which depended on levels of landownership, wealth and power. Many families within these bandings were connected through marriage, and political, religious and commercial interest. There was some stability within the top group, but a good deal of random upward and downward mobility between the other two. This was intensified by the commercial expansion taking place after 1660, the steadily improving means of travel, and the development an integrated national economy based on London. It has been suggested that the top 25,000 families exercising political power at national level were drawn from most of the nobility, and some of the greater gentry, higher clergy, and wealthy merchants, bankers, lawyers and civil servants. The main core of this coterie remained relatively stable but the overall composition was in constant flux as family fortunes changed. Below them came another fluctuating grouping drawn from some of the gentry, clergy, merchants, lawyers, professionals, civil servants, and prosperous yeomen, tradesmen and industrialists, who controlled local government in the counties and towns. Affairs at parish level were run by yeomen, leasehold farmers, husbandmen, inn keepers, tradesmen, small masters, and shopkeepers who served as tax collectors, overseers of the poor, churchwardens and village constables. Clearly, many of the elites and middle orders did not hold any form of office, but one of the major criteria of social esteem was civic responsibility, which carried with it the ability and willingness to accept office if called upon.

## 4 Wives, Widows, Courtesans and Actresses

Another way of assessing social movement and structural change is to examine the changing attitudes towards women and their role within society. The social position of elite and middle-order women underwent a marked change during the seventeenth century, especially after 1660. This has been a source of debate among historians. Some feminist writers consider that women were becoming more liberated because they had greater freedom to use their femininity and sexuality. Others think that they were more subjected to male domination and were becoming decorative status and sex objects who were used to enhance the male ego.

### a) The Uneducated Female

Certainly as far as education was concerned there was a widening gap between men and women. Boys were taught Latin grammar and a full humanistic curriculum. For girls an ability to read and write in English was considered sufficient. Apart from this, they were taught needlework, music, painting and other 'suitable' accomplishments. After the 1660s an educated woman was regarded as being socially unfashionable and a person to be ridiculed by court wits and playwrights. Although some men argued that if women were given more education they would be improved, most thought that they had been given too much freedom before and during the Civil War. Such people considered that women had become Amazons, 'to swagger, to swear, to game [gamble], to drink, to revel', and had to be restrained by sane, rational men. Not all women accepted either the prohibition on education or male superiority. In *The Female Advocate* (1689) Sarah Egerton attacked *A Late Satyr Against the Pride, Lust and Inconstancy of Women*, a poem written by Robert Gould in 1683. The 'fancy that all men are good, and fitting for heaven, because they are men; and women irreversibly damned because they are women ... is the most notorious principle, and the most unlikely that ever was maintained by any rational man'. Such protest had little effect, for as even the well educated advocate of reform for women, Mary Astell, commented in *Defence of the Female Sex*, 1697,

'They have endeavoured to train us up altogether to ease and ignorance'.

## b) Marriage

In Stuart polite society marriage was considered the only suitable career for women. This made them potentially even more socially mobile than their fathers and brothers because they took the status of their husband. There was universal social approval for the arranged marriage, while love matches were frowned upon, and beauty (unless accompanied by a large dowry) was seen as a dangerous snare for the unwary young man. Daughters were still regarded as valuable marriage pawns to cement advantageous alliances with other families. However, there was growing agreement that children should be given some say in the selection of marriage partners. Younger sons and daughters were given an increasing amount of freedom of choice. Even in the case of heirs and heiresses the fate, in 1617, of the 14-year-old Frances, daughter of Sir Edward Coke, who 'was tied to the bedposts and whipped', until she agreed to marry the Duke of Buckingham's younger brother, was becoming much less common. It became the normal practice for parents to draw up a short-list of suitable partners from which their children could choose.

Even so, heiresses were sought after avidly. Lists were drawn up by marriage brokers and circulated among the parents of young bachelors and eligible and ineligible widowers. There were plenty of cases of heiresses being kidnapped from school by unscrupulous fortune hunters, and of dishonest relatives and guardians trying to force orphans into marriage. Daughters were still seen as a marketable commodity. After 1660 this made it difficult for many members of the landed elites to compete with the wealth being generated through commerce. As Sir William Morris commented in 1672, 'There are so many merchant's daughters that weigh so many thousands that ours are commodities lying on our hands'. Sir Josiah Child, a member of the East India Company, illustrates the problem facing elite parents because when he married his daughter Rebecca to the Marquess of Worcester in 1682 he provided a dowry of £25,000.

A sign that there was growing competition for suitable husbands was that after 1660 a groom's parents were demanding larger dowries to be settled on their son, and offering smaller jointures (money settled on the bride to provide her with a living if her husband predeceased her). Previously the dowry had been about five times the jointure, but by 1700 this ratio had risen to ten to one. This made wives even more dependent on their husbands, because, under common law, a husband owned all the rest of his wife's property. A wife's situation was further complicated by the lack of any divorce procedures. Although the Church courts recognised separation, 'divorce from bed and board', neither party, whether guilty or not, was allowed to remarry, and the wife was still dependent on the husband for any financial settlement.

## c) Attitudes within Families

It must not be thought that all daughters were treated just as pieces of merchandise. Letters and diaries show that many young women were quite capable of getting their own way with their fathers. There are also plenty of examples of fathers breaking the principle of strict male settlement in their wills by ignoring nephews and cousins and leaving all their property to their daughters. It was equally common for fathers to leave money and property in trust to their daughters so that they could use it independently of their husbands. Similarly, there are many examples of love and affection between parents and children and between brothers and sisters. In her will of 1631 Lettice Knollys speaks of her dear parents, her beloved brother, and her deep respect for a friend because of his love for his children. Even the hard-headed lawyer Sir Henry Martin in his will of 1641, apart from leaving considerable sums to his beloved daughters, talks of his special affection for his granddaughter Margaret.

By the same token it must not be thought that all marriages were loveless contracts of convenience. Richard Knollys left all the residue of his estate to his 'welbeloved' wife Joan, who was to be his sole executor and to bring up the children 'in the tender love and affection of a mother'. These are the phrases and bequests that appear in so many wills of the period, and it is clear that, despite the stereotypes, a great number of marriages were based on mutual respect, love and affectionate partnership. Even the moralists approved of sex within marriage, as long as it was not taken to excess, and was avoided in hot weather. Frivolity also played its part as the Puritan minister, Henry Newcome, noted in his diary, 'spent this morning very idly in throwing water one at other'. There are now similar doubts about the accepted belief that little or no love or affection was shown towards children in the seventeenth century - an impression which is supported by a rapid increase in the production of children's clothes, books and games during the Stuart period. It is now thought that moralists argued for the strict treatment of children because they thought that parents were generally over-indulgent and spoilt their offspring.

## d) Widows

Theoretically the only time that a woman could exercise independence was when she was a widow. As elite and middle-order wives were generally younger than their husbands, widowhood frequently came relatively early. The widow was responsible for the upbringing of any young children, but was usually left a portion of her husband's estate, and had control of her jointure unless she remarried. This apparently placed young widows in a comfortable state of some freedom. The social attitude was that widows were expected to show fidelity to their dead husband by not remarrying, and spending the rest of their lives in prayer, meditation and good works. That this was far from the norm is apparent from the special praise given to Lettice, Viscountess Falkland, for not remarrying after her husband was killed in the Civil War. Indeed, it was often very difficult for wealthy widows not to remarry because they were just as avidly pursued by suitors as were heiresses. In fact it appears that many widows preferred the security of a husband, because it is estimated that more than 25 per cent remarried at least once, and 5 per cent remarried three or more times.

## e) A Shortage of Husbands

After the 1660s it became increasingly difficult for daughters of the elites and even of the middle orders to find husbands. Many of the landed elites had lost money during the Civil War and just could not find the resources to offer adequate dowries to compete with commercial wealth. As a result their daughters were forced to marry below their expectations or remain spinsters. This was not the only problem because many eligible young men had been killed in the war, forced into exile, or had gone to the colonies. For these and other reasons an increasing number of women were not marrying.

## f) Companions

The only respectable career open to unmarried women from these sections of society was to become companions or 'waiting women' to wives or widows. Samuel Pepys' younger sister, Paulina, acted as a servant companion to his wife for some time because she could not find a husband, a situation apparently unsatisfactory to all concerned. There was a considerable demand for companions, particularly as many middle-order wives, like Mrs Pepys, considered their employment a mark of social advancement. Companions had to be genteel and refined, and to be able to dance, do needlework, play a musical instrument, and preferably speak a foreign language. They were expected to help their mistresses to dress, arrange their hair, go for walks, and entertain. Frequently they were also required to look after any children and to organise the housework and cooking. In return they could hope to be paid up to £20 a year. For many it was a life of drudgery. For others, depending on the type of household in which they were employed, it could be a successful career. The most notable companion of the period was Abigail Hill who rose to be Woman of the Bedchamber to Queen Anne and was created Baroness Masham.

## g) Courtesans and Actresses

The growing immorality and eroticism of Restoration society offered less respectable opportunities for many genteel, but unmarried daughters. In a society where it was fashionable for men to have at least one mistress, a career as a courtesan offered considerable scope for advancement. It is somewhat paradoxical that at a time when women in general were regarded as being inferior, and when their activities were becoming more restricted, in some respects they became more liberated. Some Marxist feminists have defined this as women exploiting the capitalist system by using their bodies as a commodity. Being a Maid of Honour or having some other attachment at court provided the greatest opportunity for advancement, but London, provincial cities and country houses all had their own potential. Although condemned by respectable wives and matrons, courtesans were widely accepted in polite society. They were generally described as 'misses', or, as in the case of Betty Flauntit, a character in the play *The Town Fop,* 'persons of pleasure'. Respectable women and girls were always called 'Mrs', even if unmarried. Slightly less condemnatory were terms such as 'wit' or 'beauty'. Jane Sedley, the mistress of the Duke of York, who later became the Countess of Dorchester, was a 'wit'. The notorious Diana Kirk, who became the Countess of Oxford, was a 'miss'. On the other hand, the 'incomparable' Mrs Jane Myddelton was a 'beauty', although she used her sexual favours widely to earn enough to maintain herself and her husband at court.

The Restoration theatre offered similar career opportunities for less genteel girls as actresses. For the first time in 1660 the 'harmless pleasure' of having professional actresses in the theatres was permitted. Although some women took up the career in a strictly professional sense, many used the stage as a means of obtaining a suitor. Certainly many of the 'gallants' in the audience, or backstage, saw little difference between actresses, orange sellers, courtesans and prostitutes. In terms of this form of social advancement, the two most successful actresses were the rival 'beauties', the frivolous Peg Hughes, the mistress of Prince Rupert of the Rhine, and the witty Nell Gwynn, the mistress of Rupert's cousin, Charles II.

## 5 Lifestyles

By the end of the seventeenth century a distinctive patrician lifestyle was established based upon literacy, fashion and leisure. Elite status depended upon public esteem. In part this was obtained by holding public office and having authority. At the same time, a leisured, fashionable lifestyle was essential for those wishing to maintain their place in society. An ostentatious display of wealth was necessary to

*The Thames at Richmond, c.1620, Flemish school*

obtain office to retain the respect of social equals, and to secure deference from social inferiors. Lifestyle depended on a whole variety of inter-related components.

## a) Fashionable Patricians

By the early eighteenth century the elites were beginning to share a similar view about what constituted a socially acceptable way of living. The world of high fashion still centred around the court which set standards to which all those with any social pretensions aspired. Wealth, leisure, education and sophistication were the hallmarks of the gentleman. A thorough knowledge of classical history and Renaissance literature created a common bond between the male elites. It was generally expected that a gentleman had been on the Grand Tour, and stayed in the major cities of Europe. Visits to libraries, art galleries, museums and ancient sites would have given him a wide knowledge of art, sculpture, literature, architecture and antiquities. He also had to be able to discuss the theatre, science and philosophy, and to be an adept sportsman, rider, poet, musician and dancer. To be a gentleman it was necessary to be proficient in all the accomplishments, and to perform them with grace and nonchalant ease (see chapter 7).

In addition the gentleman had to be seen in the right settings. It was necessary to be noticed at court, taking the waters at Bath, backstage in the theatre, gambling on the horse races at Newmarket, or strolling in Hyde Park. Another prime requirement was a fashionable house in London for the winter season, and one in the country to entertain house parties during the summer. Such houses had to be equipped with the latest furniture and furnishings, and have salons and galleries in which to entertain and to display paintings, sculptures and antiquities. The grounds had to be landscaped and decorated with follies and classical temples by professional gardeners and architects. His establishment had to be run by a large staff of liveried flunkeys, maids, ostlers and postillions. A gentleman's wife had to be decorative, leisured and expensive, and it was preferable to be known to have an equally attractive and extravagant mistress.

## b) The Middle Orders

Although acknowledged fashionable, this way of life was neither attainable nor approved of by all members of elite and middle-order society. Many people criticised the extravagant ostentation, which was seen as a waste of resources. There were still those who supported the honest and healthy values of living in the countryside and staying at home. Foreign travel and town life were seen as decadent and undermining the sturdy, traditional English values and virtues. Even so, as the middle orders gained in wealth they also aspired to acquire social prestige and to display their new affluence. Many of the pseudo-gentry, merchants and lawyers had the wealth and connections to adopt such an opulent style of living. Other members of the middle orders tried to emulate the living standards and comfort of their social superiors in as far as their means permitted. They had to be content with putting a neo-classical facade on their old Tudor house. Their fashionable clothes were made for them out of cheaper materials by a local taylor or seamstress. They had stylish furniture made out of elm or beech instead of mahogany, and locally made china instead of imported Chinese porcelain. Elite leisure was emulated by strolling in the fashionable parks, attending horse races and the less fashionable balls and assemblies. Wives or daughters were not allowed to work, and every respectable household had to have at least one domestic servant.

In turn, servants copied the lifestyle of their employers, buying cheap imitations of fashionable goods. This is known as the 'trickle effect' and was the basis of the growth of a consumer society. By this process a taste for costly goods quickly worked its way down to even the lower rank of society. A good example of this is tea drinking which was a highly fashionable and expensive practice in the late seventeenth century. However, even quite humble country people began to acquire a taste for it because servants in the great houses collected the used tea leaves, dried them, and then sold them to the local villagers.

These issues will be re-examined and assessed in chapter 7 in the context of changing cultural values within society. At the same time a general conclusion will be made to assess the major social changes taking place within Stuart society.

---

**Making notes on** *'Society: The Landed Elites, the Pseudo-Gentry and the Middle Orders'*

The first section examines the major ways in which historians analyse the development of Stuart society. You need to make careful notes about these various approaches, and compare them with your notes from chapter 1 on the debate over social change. Section 2 looks at the way in which the elite and middle order society was changing and the major influences causing such developments. You should note carefully all the major trends and decide why and to what extent there were changes to the underlying continuity within society. The next section examines the pattern of mobility and changing perceptions of status within these sections of society in more detail. Decide to what extent landownership and authority remained the paramount criterion of status, and how far wealth and other symbols of status were becoming accepted. Section 4 discusses the debate over whether the status of women was improving or declining in the seventeenth century. You

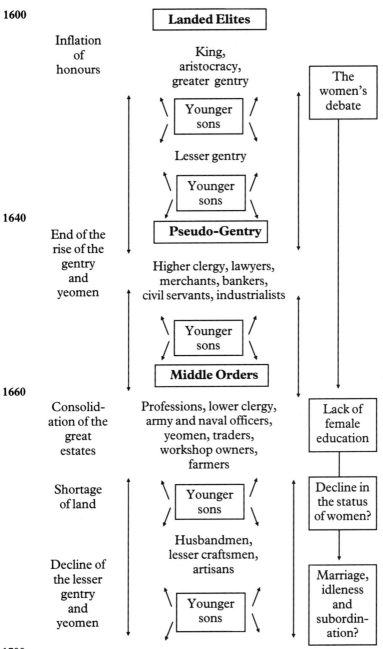

*Summary - The Landed Elites, the Pseudo-Gentry and the Middle Orders*

should note the counter arguments carefully before deciding whether women were gaining or losing prestige. The final section discusses the emergence of a distinctive patrician lifestyle and how it was emulated by those lower in the social order. You need to decide to what extent status in society was dependent upon lifestyle.

---

*Source-based questions on* 'Society: The Landed Elites, the Pseudo-Gentry and the Middle Orders'

### The Duke of Newcastle's Advice to Charles II, 1660
Carefully read the extract given on page 101. Answer the following questions.
a)  Summarise the main points of the Duke of Newcastle's advice. (5 marks)
b)  On what grounds does Newcastle object to lawyers? (2 marks)
c)  What assumptions does Newcastle make about the purposes of education? (3 marks)
d)  What evidence is there that ideas such as Newcastle's were influential in the decades after 1660? (5 marks)

CHAPTER 6

# Society: The Lower Orders

## 1 Introduction: Issues and Approaches

Stuart society has been described as still being a hierarchy of inequality. Indeed, it is considered that the disparities in society were becoming greater by 1700. This was particularly marked by the growing gulf opening up between the lower orders and the prospering elites and middle orders. It is suggested that this polarisation took several forms, and that there was increasing differentiation even within the lower orders themselves.

### a) Defining the Lower Orders

A major debating point is whether England still had a peasantry at the end of the Stuart period, or whether it had become a landless, wage-earning proletariat. If by 'peasantry' is meant rural communities predominantly consisting of small farmers (husbandmen) with up to 30 acres of land which were cultivated by family labour, England had ceased to have a peasantry by 1700. Equally, if a 'proletariat' is defined as being made up of labourers entirely dependent on wages and completely separated from the land, this is not an accurate description of the seventeenth-century lower orders either.

The lower orders were a very diverse and changing group in a state of transition. This makes it difficult to decide who should be classified as belonging to it. The problem is made worse by the fact that so many people had multiple occupations in the dual economy. For example, a small-scale farmer who also worked for wages and did some weaving in the winter could be categorised as a husbandman, a labourer or a craftsman. It also has to be decided where widows, servants and apprentices should be fitted into the structure. The issue is further complicated by variations in social structures between regions, counties and even neighbouring villages. Furthermore, people living in the closed agricultural parishes are considered to have been developing different lifestyles from those in the more industrialised open parishes (see page 124).

### b) Poverty

It is widely agreed that despite improvements in the economy after 1660 there was still widespread poverty to be found within the lower ranks of society. Gregory King estimated that in 1688 51 per cent of the population were in this category, and he described them as decreasing the wealth of the nation because they earned less than they spent. This suggests that over half the population was barely able to subsist and was on or below the poverty line. However, the degrees of poverty depended the whether an individual had access to land and common rights (see page 125) or was employed. The slow-down in the rate of population increase and the consequent fall in inflation after the 1640s is seen as making employment more available and pushing up wages. At the same time income also depended on the number of people within a family who were in employment. Furthermore, by the late seventeenth century the Elizabethan poor laws were well established and it is felt that they provided basic subsistence for the majority of those in worst need.

## c) The Sexual Division of Labour

It is possible that there was another growing division within the lower orders caused by a lessening in opportunities for working women. However, this is a matter of debate among historians. The pessimistic view is that the general deterioration in attitudes towards women adversely affected the range and quantity of work that was available to them. To an even greater extent than elite and middle-order women, those from the lower orders were denied access to education. At the best some did learn to read, but mainly training in useful (female) skills, such as spinning, knitting or domestic service, was considered to be sufficient. Lack of education, together with the prevailing belief in female mental and physical inferiority, meant that women increasingly came to be thought incapable of skilled work. Consequently, the better paid work such as ploughing, harvesting and craft work became a male preserve. At the same time the growing belief that the only place for women was the home meant that more girls were having to go into domestic service. The effect of this is considered to be that women were forced into marriage, domestic service or prostitution in order to survive. However, there is a more optimistic view of changes in the division of labour. It is suggested that because of the increasing diversity of the economy more jobs were available in a greater range of occupations. As this came at a time when the population was increasing only slowly, more single women had the opportunity to find employment. This gave them considerable economic independence, which is the reason why, by the early eighteenth century, an increasing number of women were not getting married. Both the 'pessimistic' and the 'optimistic' interpretations are plausible. Further research will need to be carried out before it will be possible to adjudicate between their competing claims.

## d) Cultural Divisions

Apart from the general difficulty of interpreting the sources (see page 16), the high percentage of lower-order illiteracy, especially among women, means that very little is known about them. In any case most of the evidence was written by members of the elites and middle orders. Consequently, historians catch only rare glimpses of life as it was actually experienced by this group. Most of the time they appear only in official records such as parish registers, taxation listings, court proceedings and poor law records, or through comments in sermons, diaries and letters. This means that such evidence is frequently distorted by official attitudes and preconceptions.

It is thought that there was a growing cultural gulf opening up between the educated sections of society and the illiterate masses. This polarisation is seen as taking several forms. There was an increasing rationalistic and optimistic belief among the elites and middle orders that mankind was capable of mastering nature and understanding the laws governing the universe. This contrasted strongly with the escapist, oral, popular culture of many of the lower orders, who feared nature and the unknown forces of magic and the spirit world. A strong clash is seen by some historians as developing between these two cultures. Popular culture is thought to have been equated with unruliness and idleness. The Puritans, the Church and the government are all seen as trying to stamp out such beliefs in order to reinforce Christianity, end disorder, and establish good working practices. There is considerable debate about how far this process had progressed by the early eighteenth century. Some historians maintain that popular culture was already disappearing, while others consider that it was still widespread even in the late nineteenth century (see page 149).

Apart from the main separation of the educated and rational from the irrational sections of society, there was growing cultural differentiation among the lower orders themselves. There is considerable debate about levels of literacy (see page 150), especially among the lower orders. It is generally agreed that illiteracy among lower-order women was virtually 100 per cent. However, it is thought that literacy among the men may have been higher than was once thought. In part this is based on the growing circulation of popular literature such as almanacs and chapbooks and ballads. It is thought that craftsmen engaged in the expanding rural industries were more likely to find it useful to read and possibly to write than agricultural workers. Consequently, it is considered that literacy levels were likely to have been higher in open industrial than in closed agricultural parishes. The spread of dissenting churches with their emphasis on bible reading may well have caused cultural divisions within individual village communities. The dissenting congregations appear to have held themselves aloof from their illiterate neighbours, whom they deemed godless and unruly (see page 149).

## 2 Lower-Order Social Structure and Mobility

As late as the mid-sixteenth century most rural and urban communities had remained very homogeneous. Yeomen and husbandmen could be found in town and country mainly engaged in farming, but also in a variety of other work, for example as butchers, clothiers, brewers and inn keepers. Although there were growing numbers of virtually landless cottagers in both town and country, they were still associated mainly with farming or agriculture-related activities. There could be considerable differences in wealth between a prosperous yeoman farming 200 acres and acting as a maltster or a brewer, and a cottager with a 4-acre garden and mainly reliant on wages for subsistence. However, communities were bound together by the need to co-operate in agricultural work, with even the urban poor going out into the countryside to help with the harvesting. Community spirit was fostered by a shared religion and culture, and by participation in festivals, holidays, sports and other leisure activities. This cohesion was strengthened by the spirit of 'good neighbourliness' whereby the villagers supported each other in times of adversity. Yeomen, although much wealthier than their neighbours, joined in the village festivities, and acted as spokesmen to the higher authorities. By 1700 this situation was changing, even if it had not changed completely, largely because of the stresses created by the growth of commercial farming, increased geographical mobility, cultural change and the pressures of government centralisation.

## a) Structural Change

Sir Thomas Smith and William Harrison writing in the 1580s (see page 98) had defined the lower orders as the great bulk of the population, who unlike the landed and urban elites and the yeomen, had no authority. By the 1690s Gregory King identified the lower orders as that section of society that consumed more than it produced. In this category he placed common soldiers and sailors, labourers and living-out servants, cottagers, paupers, vagrants and other itinerants. This is clearly a very different view of society from that of a century before. The husbandmen, farmers, tradesmen, craftsmen and artisans who all previously formed part of the lower orders were now separated into the wealth creating section of society. The former close-knit community appears to have fragmented. What is difficult to decide was how far this apparent separation applied in villages and parishes all over the country.

    Definitions by modern historians do not altogether resolve this question. Lawrence Stone defines the lower orders as living-out labourers, living-in servants, apprentices and dependents on charity, while David Cressy classifies them as labourers and servants. This suggests that an increasing gap existed between the unskilled labouring poor and the skilled artisan and self-employed husbandmen and craftsmen who had previously been the core of the peasantry. However, there is the difficulty that there were considerable economic differences within any of these groups and that individual circumstances could change very quickly. Many yeomen and husbandmen were coming under increasing economic pressure after the 1660s because of the need to invest and adopt new methods (see page 53). It is calculated that a farmer needed at least 50 acres in order to have enough resources to be able to survive a poor season. Many within this group were being forced into other occupations. Although the economy was expanding, giving opportunities for wider employment and a growing range of craft activities, it was liable to sharp fluctuations. The long period of wars between 1690 and 1713 (see page 81) depressed trade causing unemployment and putting clothiers, industrialists, tradesmen and craftsmen under pressure. Many people from the self-employed, wealth creating groups at the bottom of the middle orders could easily be forced downwards into destitution at any time. This meant that there was a substantial fluctuating section of society between the middle orders and the labouring poor from which there was constant upward and downward social mobility.

The hearth tax (see page 18) returns for Stanford in Vale in Berkshire help to illustrate the nature of this narrow dividing line. In 1662 the tax return records the village as having 96 households. Of these, 27 were excused paying any tax on the grounds of poverty. This represents 28 per cent of the villagers, and corresponds closely to the estimated national poverty level of 30 per cent. All these cottages had one hearth, apart from two which had two fireplaces, and all were worth less than 20 shillings in annual rent. It is considered that families living in such cottages were likely to be just on or below the poverty line. If this is the case, another 36 Stanford cottages had 2 or fewer fireplaces, indicating that a further 38 per cent of the villagers were only just above the poverty line. Another 20 families lived in houses with 3 fireplaces, which is considered to have indicated a comfortable standard of living, while the remainder who had houses with between 4 and 12 hearths were prosperous. The 1664 returns show how the picture could change in just 2 years. The same 27 families were exempt on the grounds of poverty, which supports the view that the numbers in receipt of poor relief remained relatively constant. However, the number of families taxed on 2 hearths or below had risen to 42, 47 per cent of the village population. Among the villagers only William Kemble appears to have improved his position, being taxed on 2 hearths in 1662 and on 5 in 1664. William Basset seems to have experienced the greatest downturn in fortune, as he paid tax on only 2 hearths in 1664 in contrast to the 7 on which he was assessed in 1662.

These returns are also helpful in illustrating another aspect of the social structure. One of the ways of distinguishing the bottom tier of the middling ranks from the lower orders was that they exercised authority at parish level. The tax return for Stanford was affirmed for the county authorities by John Southby and Roger Packer, who were both members of the local gentry. At the parish level it was signed by the parson, Giles Bingley, who had a house in the village with three hearths. It was also signed by John Bennett and Giles Tawyer who were churchwardens and overseers of the poor. However, while Tawyer, who had a house with five fireplaces, clearly belonged to the middle orders, Bennett with a one-hearthed cottage seems more akin to the lower orders. The same applies to the two other signatories, the village constables, Richard Church and James Cox, who had cottages with only one and two hearths respectively. This shows the problems of social definition, especially as it could vary widely between counties and parishes.

## b) Diversity

Improved communications meant that people were moving around the country and abroad more freely. Such migration is seen as undermining the traditional communities and speeding up the process of social change. It is estimated that the turn-over in village population was some 40 per cent every 10 years. The ease with which people from all sections of the population could move about despite the Settlement Act (see page 32), is well illustrated by Richard Gough's account of his own Shropshire village, *The History of Myddle* (1701). People from the village travelled to London, Wales and all over the Midlands, often to settle elsewhere, and then moved back again. Improved travel facilities also helped to create changes in the pattern of population distribution with the expansion of rural industry in the Midlands and the North, and the emergence of 'open' and 'closed' parishes (see page 57).

   Although open industrial parishes were more common in forest than in fielden areas, they could be found in any part of the country. In agricultural Oxfordshire the neighbouring parishes of Holton and Wheatley were respectively closed and open. Holton was enclosed and the land divided into three or four large leasehold farms. In addition a number of cottages had been demolished to make way for a deer park surrounding the manor house. The number of cottagers was restricted to those needed to work the manor farms, and no ale houses were permitted. The villagers had to attend church regularly, dressed in the clothes of their calling, and sit in a hierarchy of precedence on the benches opposite the pews occupied by the lord of the manor and his family. In contrast, Wheatley still had open fields and commons and there was no dominant lord of the manor. The village was noted for the number of its ale houses, coaching inns and the high level of drunkenness and lawlessness. In addition to numerous small holdings, there was a variety of industries, such as brick making, quarrying, and metal working. These are two very contrasting communities, and their counterparts could be found all over England.

   Urban populations, particularly London's, were increasing. This, it is suggested, was having an effect on the social structure as more people were becoming disassociated from the countryside. However, too much stress should not be placed on this because agriculture in various forms still dominated the economy. Most towns were too small to be separated from the countryside, and even in London cattle and sheep grazed in the parks, and milkmaids continued to sell fresh milk from their pails in the heart of the city. This is not to say that the growth of London did not influence the way in which the social structure was evolving. The penetration of traditional communities is seen as being a major force in creating change. London as the centre of the national economy had begun to have a considerable influence on the whole country. Charles Davenant, another of the many emerging political economists, commented in 1695 that there was 'not an acre of land in the country, be it never so distant, that is not in some degree bettered by the growth of trade and riches of that city'. Equally, central legislation and the growing bureaucracy of local government were intruding into communities and breaking down regional and local differences in social structure and organisation. However, it is still thought that this took the form of a ripple-effect, and that the further a community was from London, or a large city, the less it was affected.

## 3 Poverty and the Labouring Poor

The improvement in the economy meant that prospects for employment were much improved after the 1660s. This, linked with the slow-down in population growth, a reduction in the rate of inflation, and a rise in wage levels should have brought a marked improvement in living standards for the lower orders. However, Gregory King's view that a large part of this section of society lived on or below the poverty line is shared by many historians. The reason may well have been that the loss of access to land and other communal rights out-weighed in real terms the benefits of higher employment. In any case, there was still a considerable amount of under-employment because much of the work was seasonal or casual. Furthermore, as the economy was becoming complex and dependent on overseas commerce, it was more prone to fluctuations which might cause widespread temporary unemployment. Dependence on wages did not carry with it the same security that access to common land and the right to graze a cow and some pigs had a century previously.

### a) Vagrancy and Settlement

A.L. Beier in *Masterless Men: The Vagrancy Problem in England 1560-1640* (1985) and P. Slack in *Poverty and Policy in Tudor and Stuart England* (1988) both agree, although from different viewpoints, that poverty and vagrancy were under control after 1660. Greater availability of employment after the 1660s is seen as reducing the need for long-distance vagrancy among young adolescents seeking work. In any case the problem had been eased because large numbers of potential young vagrants had left England to settle in the colonies. At the same time it is thought that many young men were taken up by the press gangs to serve in the rapidly expanding army and navy.

The Settlement Act of 1662 (see page 32) made it easier for people to settle in a parish because they had only to be resident for 40 days to receive a certificate instead of 3 years as had previously been the case. An amending Act in 1697 eased the situation still further by establishing that settlers could not be moved on within 40 days unless they were a burden to the parish. This meant that people could much more readily move and settle over short distances, and so created a mobility in the labour force that had previously been lacking. Moreover, as certificate holders had the right to be supported by any parish through which they passed, the threat of destitution prior to finding work had been reduced.

## b) Parish Relief

Although the situation had improved this did not mean that there was not still widespread poverty. The Elizabethan poor law of 1601 which provided relief for the impotent poor was functioning effectively by 1700. Under the Act urban and rural parishes had to provide support for the disabled, the aged, especially widows and widowers, and young children and orphans. The amount spent on poor relief rose sharply

---

Report of Derbyshire Justices on Their Proceedings, 1631

1 We have taken care that the lords and parishioners of every town [township meaning village] relieve the poor thereof, and they are not suffered to straggle or beg up and down either in their parishes or elsewhere. But such poor as have transgressed have been
5 punished according to law, and the impotent there are carefully relieved. We have made special inquiry of such poor children as are fit to be bound apprentices to husbandry and otherwise, and of such as are fit to take apprentices ... We have one House of Correction at Ashborn within our wapentake, [hundred] which is
10 near the town prison, where such as are committed [gaoled for vagrancy] are kept to work.

---

between 1600 and 1700. The cost in 1610 was about £35,000 a year, had risen to £200,000 by 1650, and reached at least £350,000 by 1700. Given the increased employment and the sharp drop in the number of young children in need of care, it is thought that this was sufficient to provide reasonable care for the impotent poor. Deep poverty (absolute destitution) was virtually eradicated.

The number of those in shallow poverty, (in danger of suffering some destitution for all or part of their lives) at best remained constant, and may well have increased. In part this was the result of the greater fluctuations in the economy which might cause people to be thrown out of work. At the same time seasonal under-employment could easily put many families into temporary difficulties. Illness, accidents, or the death of a partner were everyday occurrences that could put otherwise hard-working families in need. Such problems were often aggravated by loss of traditional rights such as gathering firewood and gleaning, and a reduction in hospitality and the provision of free meals. It is estimated that some 80 per cent of the total relief went to the able bodied in temporary distress. This took the form of short-term payments and doles until a family or individual was able to become self-supporting again.

The potential difference in living standards between a relatively poor husbandman and even a semi-skilled labourer were quite considerable. In 1635 the inventory of Agnes Bagges of Hinton Waldris in Berkshire, who had been described as a poor widow in other documents, indicates that she lived in some comfort. She had a farmhouse with a hall, a bedroom, two other rooms, a kitchen and a milk house, and kept cattle, pigs and chickens. The value of all her goods and chattels amounted to £49 17s 0d, £28 18s 1d of which came from the farm animals and crops, but she only had 1s in her purse. The inventory of John Medowe, a ship's carpenter, who died at Ipswich in 1627 shows a marked contrast. He lived in one room and all his worldly goods were worth only £8 0s 1d, £5 of which was the value of his clothes, but he did have 6s 9d in his purse.

It is thought that the success of the poor relief system was that by 1700 it was capable of preventing severe destitution. The lower orders were no longer seen as a threat as they had been in the previous century. Social deference was reinforced by the payment of welfare. Householders did not mind paying the poor rates because it gave them security, and respectability by distinguishing them from the poor. As a result parish rates were generally kept high, and payments were generous. This was especially true because some ratepayers, even some of the parish officials, such as those at Stanford in the Vale, realised that they might through some misfortune become recipients themselves. The system, although bureaucratic, never became impersonal because it was organised at a parish level. Relief was handed out by officials who knew most of the beneficiaries personally, and some of whom might be their own relatives. In many places the old traditional custom of good neighbourliness and mutual help had been replaced by the sympathetic attitudes of the parish authorities.

## 4 Attitudes Towards Work and Lower-Order Leisure Preference

In contrast to the generosity of provision for those in actual need was the censorious attitude of many employers and commentators towards the supposed idleness of the lower orders. By 1700 the able-bodied poor were becoming seen by the elites and middle orders as an asset, whose labour created wealth in the economy, provided that they could be persuaded to work. Sermons emphasised that poverty was a condition ordained by God, and that it was the duty of the poor to work, while idleness was sinful. Such attitudes were not new. Part of the driving force behind the Tudor Church of England's attempt to 'reform manners' had included the abolition of festivals and saints' days, which were seen to encourage idleness, drunkeness and unruly behaviour.

### a) Working Hours

The Statute of Artificers of 1563 established working hours as being from 5 am to 8 pm from the middle of March to the middle of September, and during daylight hours for the remainder of the year. It was also stipulated that only two and half hours a day be allowed for eating and drinking. In practice this legislation, although in force until 1813, had little effect. For those whose work was associated with agriculture, hours were regulated by the seasons and weather conditions. Rural industry, with its putting out system (see page 57) meant that most people were working in their own homes at their own pace. In any case, most people had at least two jobs if not more, and these could not be fitted into a regular pattern. Even in the larger urban workshops hours appear to have been very flexible, with long breaks for drinking, and in some cases, ale boys were employed to keep the workforce regularly supplied. In any case, many urban industries closed down during the late-summer to allow the workers to help with the harvesting.

### b) Leisure Preference

Irregular working hours and seasonal unemployment and under-employment meant that there was no fixed pattern of work. This is not to say that the majority of people did not work hard and for long hours, but it did frequently mean that if they did not feel like working they stayed away. This leisure preference was well illustrated by an anonymous satirical poem of 1639:

> You know that Monday is Sunday's brother;
> Tuesday is such another;

Wednesday you must go to Church and pray;
Thursday is half-holiday;
On Friday it is too late to begin to spin;
The Saturday is half-holiday again.

The universal practice of treating Mondays as a holiday led to it becoming known as St Monday, an unofficial saint's day.

Lower-order work practices and leisure was closely linked with popular culture (see page 139). People were very superstitious and frequently did not go to work if it was one of their unlucky days, or if there was some other portent or omen. Festivals, carnivals, village ales, wakes and weddings, which were a central part of community culture, were also regarded as holidays. Local sporting events such as football matches, cock fighting, and horse racing were equally seen as perfectly good reasons for not going to work. However, the major cause of lost working time in the official view was the ale house, which formed the centre of village activities. The Derbyshire magistrates who had so carefully provided for the poor in 1631, noted that they had closed down over a third of the ale houses in their district to prevent idleness and drunkenness.

Such behaviour, which was regarded as feckless escapism, was the major cause of irritation among commentators. The refusal of large sections of the lower orders to work longer than was necessary to provide for their immediate needs was seen as irrational. This was particularly true by the late seventeenth century when economic realism and increasing commercialisation demanded work discipline. Richard Baxter in his *Poor Husbandman's Advocate* (1691) was very sympathetic to what he saw as the poor but hard-working husbandmen who had to sell all their best produce to pay the rent and could feed their families only on curdled milk and rye bread. At the same time, he was totally dismissive of the labouring poor, calling them 'the rabble that cannot read'. The growth of economic rationalism among writers at this time led to a growing feeling that the provision of welfare apart from the

---

Daniel Defoe, Giving Alms No Charity, 1704

1 1 There is in England more labour than hands to perform it, and consequently a want of people, not of employment.
2 No man in England, of sound limbs and senses, can be poor merely for want of work.
5 3 All our workhouses, corporations and charities for employing the poor, and setting them to work ... are, and will be public nuisances, mischiefs to the nation which serve to the ruin of families and the increase of the poor ...
There is a general taint of slothfulness [idleness] upon our poor,
10 there is nothing more frequent, than for an Englishman to work till

he has got his pocket full of money, and then go and be idle, or perhaps drunk, till it is all gone, and perhaps he himself in debt; and ask him in his cups what he intends, he will tell you honestly, he will drink as long as it lasts, and then go to work for more.

---

impotent and destitute was a mistake. There was an increasing feeling that the imposition of greater work discipline on the labouring poor would improve economic efficiency.

## 5 Women at Work

The working lives of women are seen by some historians to have begun to deteriorate by the beginning of the eighteenth century. For others the slowing down of population growth and the expansion of the economy is considered to have offered greater opportunities for single women to find employment. The reconciliation of these two extremes is difficult, but there is evidence to support both points of view.

### a) Training and Finding Work

The hardening of male attitudes towards women during the seventeenth century, especially after 1660 (see page 100), certainly had repercussions on lower-order women. The strengthening of the belief in women's physical and mental inferiority made it harder for them to obtain skilled, well-paid work. Restrictions in education after 1660 also made it very difficult for lower-order women to obtain any formal education. It is estimated that there was virtually 100 per cent illiteracy among this section of society in most areas of the country. In addition it became harder for adolescent girls to obtain skilled training as apprentices, or as servants in industry or husbandry. This meant that women became regarded as a cheap source of labour. The better-paid skilled and heavier jobs in industry and agriculture became male preserves, while women were expected to do the more monotonous and repetitive work, such as spinning and knitting or weeding and hoeing.

The growing demand for servants meant that domestic service was becoming a major area of employment for lower-order girls. In the sixteenth century the over-employment of domestic servants had been frowned on as wasteful ostentation. At the same time most domestic servants had been married men and women. By the end of the seventeenth century having a large number of servants was regarded as fashionable. It was also seen as an ideal training for adolescent girls, who provided a cheap labour force. This 'feminisation of domestic service' is seen by many historians as further evidence of the worsening in the status of women in that it reinforced the concept that housework was the only suitable type of female employment.

## b) Single Women

It is undoubtedly true that the development of domestic service, and the growth in the textile trades did offer considerable employment opportunities for women. There were also increasing openings to be found in such areas as dressmaking, hairdressing, laundering, as well as in occupations connected with the rapid expansion in travel and leisure. The demographic evidence suggests that women were marrying later and that by the end of the seventeenth century more were remaining single. What is less certain is that this was not just a reaction to the adverse economic conditions in the period 1600-40, and to the lack of available partners, rather than a desire for independence. It is doubtful if any of the available work was sufficiently well paid to give single women real economic independence.

In any case, social attitudes put considerable pressure on lower-order women to marry. Disapproval for single women remained very strong as it was felt that a woman's place was within a family under the control of father, husband or master. Another difficulty was that parish authorities saw unattached women as being likely to become a burden to the poor rates. The term spinster, denoting a single woman, became one of abuse. This was because spinning was a low-paid occupation and was associated with poverty.

Another disadvantage was that the belief in female sexual voracity meant that the authorities frequently regarded young single women as potential prostitutes, or at the best liable to become pregnant. This was coupled with the sexual double standard that placed the blame of pregnancy outside marriage on the woman rather than the man. Although the demographic statistics seem to point to a relatively low illegitimacy rate, contemporary evidence suggests that it was by no means uncommon. In writing about Myddle, Richard Gough frequently refers to girls having become pregnant and running away. He says of one of his neighbours, Elizabeth Tyler: 'She was more commemorable for her beauty than her chastity', while her daughter Mary had the same reputation, and 'her daughters are so infamous for their lewdness, that I even loathe to say more of them'. This may well have reflected the way in which better employment prospects and greater ease of travel was breaking down community values. It appears that in a section of society where premarital pregnancy was common many young men who would normally have married their pregnant partner left to settle elsewhere. Young domestic servants also faced the problem of sexual advances from their master or his sons, suspicion of which, let alone pregnancy, generally resulted in them being thrown out on to street by the wife. Such deserted girls were frequently driven out of the parish.

The moral laxity of post-Restoration England generally made prostitution socially acceptable. This and the growing number of deserted girls often created difficulties for parish relief. The problem faced by the authorities is well illustrated by Richard Gough's comment on two daughters of another of his neighbours who were 'as impudent whores as any in this country: one of them has two bastards, and she being run out of the county they are both maintained by the parish'. Some deserted girls went to the nearest large town to try to find respectable employment, which was often difficult in their condition. Frequently they had to find refuge in the workhouse or to join other, more willing recruits in organised urban prostitution. This supports the point made by some feminist historians that it was becoming easier for women to use their bodies as a commodity. In financial terms prostitution could be more lucrative than many other respectable female occupations: 2 pence a day for spinning, 4 pence a day for agricultural work, and £2 to £4 a year with board for domestic service. As Samuel Pepys phrased it even common prostitutes could earn 6 pence a 'bout' in the country and 1s 8d in London.

## c) Women in the Home

One of the problems for lower-order women was that the home was increasingly not necessarily the place of work. When the characteristic home had been a farm run mainly by family labour, housework had been part of the wife's economic contribution to the family. This remained true for wives on both large and small farms, who continued to organise the house, supervise the servants, feed the farm labourers, and often run the dairy and look after chickens.

To a certain extent the same was true in many areas of cottage industry. The husband often worked in the house as a weaver or in some other craft, but he might equally well be employed outside as a labourer, miner, or in a workshop. The wife and young children worked at home in various activities such as spinning, carding, stocking knitting, lace making or glove making to earn extra family income. Generally, in these cases the housework was part of the daily routine. However, when the members of the family all worked outside the home, housework became a non-economic chore which wives were expected to do after they had finished work. Even by the early eighteenth century a distinction was becoming recognised between male and female work. The concept which became established was that men had the right to better-paid employment because they were the main provider for the family. Women's economic contribution became minimalised down to 'pin money', emphasising their subordinate role both at work and in the family.

## 6 Conclusion

Despite recent research, much less is known about the lower orders than about other sections of society so that any conclusions must still be tentative and open to debate. It is becoming clearer that by the late seventeenth century the lower orders were no longer just all the population who did not belong to the landed and urban elites and the yeomanry. Husbandmen, leasehold farmers, and skilled craftsmen had become part of the middle orders. The lower orders were made up of the landless labouring (able-bodied) poor and the impotent poor. This suggests that if the lower orders could previously be called a peasantry made up of smallholders, this was no longer the case by 1700.

A widening economic gap was opening up between this group and most of the rest of society. Abject poverty among the aged, young children and the disabled seems to have been overcome through improved parish poor relief. Similarly, the Settlement Act of 1662 and improved employment opportunities had reduced vagrancy. Nevertheless, many of the labouring masses lived on or below the poverty line. However, it is thought that there was more generous provision of parish relief for the able-bodied poor. This is considered to have brought greater social stability and ended the fear of lower-order riot and rebellion among the elites that had been so prevalent in the sixteenth century. In any case there was considerable diversity because income depended upon where families lived, what opportunities were available to them, and how many of the family were in employment. Nor was the dividing line between the lower orders and the bottom of the middle orders clear-cut. Husbandmen, tradesmen and skilled artisans could easily slide into poverty, while labouring families might prosper.

The question of living standards is equally open to differing interpretations. Because of the slowing in the rate of population growth more employment was available, inflation was lower and wages were increasing. This should have given the lower orders greater spending power. However, they were criticised for having a leisure preference and earning only sufficient for their immediate needs. Yet, even if they were spending money on beer, gin, tobacco, gambling and leisure, rather than buying cheap consumer goods from the local shop, they were still contributing to economic growth and expanding the consumer society.

There were also widening gaps opening up within the lower orders. The most marked differences are seen to be between those living in open industrial parishes and towns and the inhabitants of closed agricultural parishes. Settlement and employment opportunities were much better in the former, which made them attractive to migrant workers who saw them as a chance to improve their living standard through higher wages. In closed parishes wages were lower but, as they were linked to parish relief, provided greater security. Such diversity is considered to have been accentuated by growing cultural differences. There is thought to have been not just a separation of the rational elites and middle orders from the irrational lower orders, but also between the literate and illiterate sections of the lower orders themselves. This issue will be discussed in more detail in the next chapter.

***Making notes on** 'Society: The Lower Orders'*

The opening section examines the problem of defining the lower orders, and the key issues of poverty, the position of working women and changes to lower-order culture. These are fundamental to an understanding of the lower orders, and you should note all the arguments very carefully. Section 2 discusses the ways in which lower-order society was changing. Remember it is still argued by some people that England had a peasant society in 1700, and you should have clear ideas on this point. The next section looks at improvements in poor relief and changing attitudes towards poverty. Although the impotent poor were reasonably well provided for, the numbers of the labouring poor are thought to have been increasing, and you should decide why this was happening at a time of rising living standards. The last section discusses the debate over the status of working women. You need to note the various arguments very carefully before deciding whether working women, especially if they were single, were worse or better off by 1700.

***Answering essay questions on Stuart Society***

Most people working in the social sciences need to create 'models' in order to make sense of the situations they are studying. Social historians are no different. One of their central tasks is to construct a model of whatever society they are studying. However, because social historians attempt to explain societies over a period of time they are very much involved in describing change and the reasons for it. Hence examiners setting questions on the topic of Stuart Society are primarily interested in models, definitions, and the 'what?' and 'why?' of change. Study the following questions to check that this is so.

1   In what ways did the structure of English society alter during the seventeenth century?
2   Did the status of women in England improve or worsen during the seventeenth century?
3   'During the Stuart period the ownership of land ceased to be the main determinant of social status in England.' Do you agree.
4   Why did differentiation within the lower orders increase in late seventeenth-century England?
5   What were the effects of changing attitudes towards education in Stuart England?
6   Discuss the view that 'between 1600 and 1700 the English elite's perception of the poor changed dramatically'.

Two of these questions make major assumptions that need to be

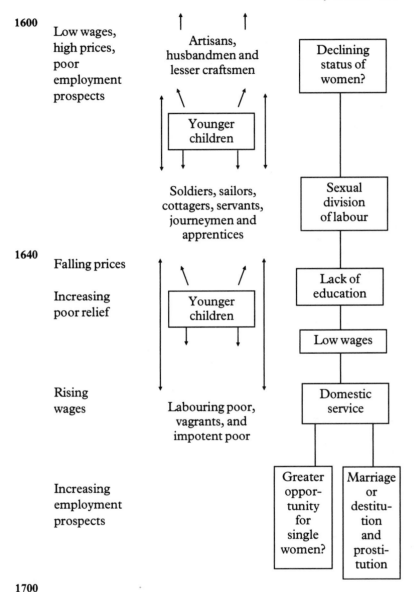

**1600**

Low wages, high prices, poor employment prospects

Artisans, husbandmen and lesser craftsmen

Younger children

Soldiers, sailors, cottagers, servants, journeymen and apprentices

Declining status of women?

**1640**

Falling prices

Increasing poor relief

Younger children

Rising wages

Labouring poor, vagrants, and impotent poor

Sexual division of labour

Lack of education

Low wages

Domestic service

Increasing employment prospects

Greater opportunity for single women?

Marriage or destitution and prostitution

**1700**

*Summary - Society: The Lower Orders*

explored when answering them. Which are they? Several of the
questions require answers which display an understanding of the
differing views of historians. With which question is this most evidently
the case?

---

*Source-based questions on 'Society: The Lower Orders'*

### 1 Operation of the Poor Law, 1631
Carefully read the extract from the report of the Derbyshire JPs, given
on page 126. Answer the following questions.
a)  What is meant by 'the impotent there are carefully relieved' (line 0)?
    (2 marks)
b)  Why were the JPs keen that the poor should not be allowed 'to
    straggle or beg up and down either in their parishes or elsewhere'?
    (3 marks)
c)  Explain the reported action for dealing with poor children and the
    thinking that lay behind it. (5 marks)
d)  Why was the JPs' report being made? How should these reasons
    affect the way in which historians interpret the report? (5 marks)

### 2 Attitudes towards the Poor
Carefully read the poem and the extract from Defoe's writings, given on
pages 129 and 130. Answer the following questions.
a)  What message is the poem attempting to give? (2 marks)
b)  What assumptions lie behind the poem's central idea? (3 marks)
c)  Explain the argument that Defoe is advancing in his three numbered
    points. (4 marks)
d)  What were likely to be the effects of the attitudes displayed by the
    poem and by the last paragraph of the Defoe extract? (6 marks)

# CHAPTER 7

# Cultural Change

## 1 Introduction: Issues and Approaches

Cultural developments are important in trying to assess change and continuity within a society. There were a number of cultural changes taking place during the seventeenth century which are important to the understanding of Stuart England. London and the court were having a significant influence on fashionable society. This in turn was changing the way people lived and thought, and affected the lifestyles (see page 113) and leisure pursuits of both the elites and the middle orders. Changing attitudes towards education and the growing rationality of thought among the intellectuals created a more progressive outlook. A major consequence of this was the 'scientific revolution' of the late seventeenth century. It has been suggested that these developments among the elites and middle orders were opening up an ever widening gap between them and the illiterate lower orders who continued their belief in their traditional popular culture.

Although there is general agreement among historians that these changes were taking place, there is considerable disagreement about the extent of the changes and the nature of their impact on society. The seventeenth century used to be seen as a time when there was a break with traditional ideas and values. Indeed, it has even been suggested that the 1650s marked the real end of the Middle Ages, and that Restoration England saw the beginning of modern rational thinking. Although many writers have not agreed that the changes were this dramatic, it is clearly the case that Stuart society was undergoing some important cultural changes. However, most historians now see these as forming part of an evolutionary process in which many old ideas were retained alongside the new 'scientific' rationality.

### a) London as a Cultural Centre

It is undoubtedly true that London through its size, and because of its attraction as a political, educational and social centre did have a great influence on cultural and social development in Stuart England. However, it is now thought that the influence exerted by the capital and the court was not consistent throughout the whole of the seventeenth century. Under James I and Charles I the court had a paramount role in establishing fashion in the visual arts. Inigo Jones, Ben Jonson and Sir Anthony Van Dyck, through the masque, architecture, drama and painting, placed England on an equal footing with the great baroque courts of Western Europe. However, the high cost of what has been called 'the top heavy Renaissance court' (see page 4) made it unpopular with tax payers. This artistic phase was once considered to have been ended by the Civil War and the austerity of the Interregnum and to have re-emerged only after 1660. However, some historians have doubted whether the Commonwealth period was as artistically sterile or the Restoration as culturally productive as was once thought. The development of the London fashionable 'season' associated with the court undoubtedly had a considerable influence on polite society. It was thought that this was of paramount importance to the 'urban renaissance'.

The development of leisure towns, such as Bath and Shrewsbury, and the transformation of provincial capitals and county towns into social centres for the local elites was once thought to have emanated directly from the capital. However, it is now considered that this was a response to local needs as well an emulation of London fashion and amenities. In any case, it is thought that after 1660 political power moved away from the court and Parliament back to the aristocracy and greater gentry, and that this strengthened county societies and helped them to retain their own identities.

## b) Education and Rationality

The expansion of education after 1540 is considered to have ended by the 1660s. After the Restoration access to education was limited for all women and the lower orders because of the fear that it gave them too much freedom (see page 101). At the same time, education became less fashionable among the male elites and there was a decline in the numbers attending and taking degrees at university and a drop in the number of public and grammar schools being founded. Universities were seen primarily as finishing schools where young men mixed with their social equals and were given private tuition in useful accomplishments such as speaking French and Italian, dancing and fencing. At the same time the attempts to reform the curriculum proposed during the Commonwealth (see page 101) were abandoned after the Restoration. Schools and universities continued to teach grammar and, predominantly, humanistic history and classics. It was this thorough grounding in classical literature and history that became the hallmark of male polite society.

Such limitations have led to doubts being expressed about the extent of the spread of rationality among even the male elites and middle orders. There was certainly a growing confidence in humanity's ability to master nature, and a belief in progress. Yet, it is thought that there was still a widespread acceptance of aspects of traditional culture, such as alchemy and astrology. Although there is evidence of increasing male literacy based on the ability to sign documents, some reservations are now being expressed about the validity of this method of assessment. It is questioned whether a signature indicates the ability to read and write. Furthermore, it is suggested that for many people the ability to read might have been just a mechanical skill which did not necessarily show real understanding or literacy.

## c) The 'Scientific Revolution'

The mid-seventeenth century has been seen as a cultural watershed, marking a distinct break between traditional ideas and the beginning of 'modern' rationality. The most notable sign of this change was considered to have been the late Stuart 'scientific revolution', symbolised by the establishment of the Royal Society in 1662 to promote and apply fresh ideas. The new intellectual approach used empirical reasoning which was based on observation and experiment to prove a hypothesis. This is considered to have replaced traditional methods based on accepted truth and the classical Greek method of logical development of theory. Francis Bacon was the first major English exponent of this inductive thinking, which was taken up later in the century by people like Isaac Newton and Robert Boyle. Such developments were thought to have been linked with the Puritan ideology which favoured educational reform and the practical application of scientific and economic ideas.

However, recently there have been increasing doubts about whether there was such a radical break in seventeenth-century thinking and outlook and about its association with Puritanism. It is now thought that the process was much more evolutionary and that many traditional characteristics continued into the eighteenth century. In addition, it is felt that fresh approaches developed naturally out of humanistic thinking rather than out of new Puritan ideas. It is considered that even some of the leading intellectuals, such as Bacon and Newton, were less scientific in their approach than was once thought. Moreover, the role of the Royal Society in promoting significant advances is now questioned, especially as many of its members continued to retain their belief in such ideas as alchemy, mysticism and witchcraft.

## d) Popular Culture

By popular culture is meant the traditional and largely oral ideas about subjects such as magic, and the leisure pursuits and rituals still practised by the lower orders. Until the English Reformation this had been the culture shared by all sections of society, and it had blended in with the beliefs and rituals of the old medieval Church. But it is thought that, from the 1530s onwards, popular culture was under attack from Protestant reformers and intellectuals who regarded it as pagan and as harbouring Catholic beliefs and practices. Tudor and Stuart governments also attacked it because they saw it as a cause of idleness, drunkenness and disorder. At the same time, the growth of lay education from the end of the fifteenth century, and especially after 1540, is considered to have caused a separation of elite from popular culture. Elite culture is seen as being based on literacy and rationality of thought, while popular culture is thought of as being based on oral tradition, irrationality and escapism.

Although some historians maintain that popular culture was beginning to disappear by the end of the seventeenth century, others consider that in some ways it was being strengthened. There was growth of lower-order male literacy up to the 1660s, which was maintained thereafter by self-education. This is indicated by the high sales of popular literature such as chapbooks, almanacs, ballads, histories and romances. Such demand is thought to have strengthened popular culture because oral traditions were written down and conserved in this literature, and to have helped to sustain it well into the nineteenth century. It is also doubted whether the growth of scientific rationality led to complete cultural separation between the lower orders and the rest of society. Large sections of the elites and middle orders continued to practise many of the traditional customs and to participate in sporting and leisure activities with the lower orders. Even leading scientific intellectuals such as Isaac Newton continued to believe in alchemy and other traditional ideas.

## 2 London as a Centre of Cultural and Urban Influence

London and the court are considered to have been centres for the dissemination of cultural ideas throughout the seventeenth century. The court was the focus of fashion, attracting the elites and other social aspirants, particularly as communications and transport facilities improved. Apart from the permanent courtiers, officials, musicians and artists who lived in the districts around Westminster, many of the provincial elites had houses or lodged in London for the winter season. This is seen is as creating an interchange of urban and courtly values, and as having encouraged the development of increasingly sophisticated amenities in London itself. At the same time, when the visitors returned to their rural residences they began to introduce these values into county society and to demand improved local amenities. This can be seen as another example of the 'trickle effect' (see page 116) with ideas filtering down through society and spreading out from London into the provinces. However, it is doubted that this had created a national culture by 1700 and it is thought that provincial societies continued to retain some of their own distinctive characteristics.

### a) London as a Centre of Cultural Influence

London through its very size clearly had a very significant influence on England during the seventeenth century. It is calculated to have meant that one person in six of the entire population either lived in or visited the capital at some time during the course of the century. London's position as the major European entrepôt made it a very cosmopolitan centre, attracting not only people but ideas from all over the world. The court and the winter 'season' lured the elites because to be seen in this environment was an essential prerequisite of social recognition. For this reason the aristocracy and greater gentry either built or rented houses in the fashionable West End. The Inns of court still recruited large numbers of students because of their proximity to the court, theatres, and the other less educational attractions of city life. Merchants and their agents from the provinces and abroad came to London as a centre of commerce, banking and insurance.

As a centre of opulence and display London had a considerable influence on the provincial elites. Even by 1630 it is estimated that two-thirds of the aristocracy and several hundred of the gentry owned or leased houses in London. This meant that there was a rapid development of luxury housing. Rubens commented in 1629 that, 'The first thing to be noted is that all the leading nobles live on a sumptuous scale and spend money lavishly, so that the majority of them are in debt'. In 1629 the Earl of Bedford began developing Covent Garden as an area of high-class housing. The Strand, where Inigo Jones lived, Richmond, Chelsea, Kensington and Tottenham were noted for their aristocratic palaces. Blackfriars, Lincoln's Inn Fields, Soho and High Holborn all became centres of fashionable housing. Such dwellings provided all the latest comfort and sophistication that might be expected from close proximity to the court. This is what is seen as a prime source of cultural cross-fertilisation between London, the court and the provinces.

Wealthy courtiers, visiting landowners and the City elites all expected London to provide a wide range and a high standard of amenities. The Great Fire of 1666 enabled the replacement of many narrow streets and much of the overcrowded medieval housing by broad thoroughfares and elegant stone-built houses. Leisure parks such as Hyde Park enabled the fashionable to stroll and to show off their clothes, their wit, their wives or their latest mistresses. At the same time they could admire the flower beds, the glasshouses full of exotic plants, and the aviaries with tropical birds. Alternatively they could visit one of the many coffee houses to exchange gossip, or drink tea in the salons of sophisticated hostesses. The theatres and other places of recreation, ranging from cock fighting and bull baiting to musical evenings and meetings of the Antiquarian Society, provided entertainment throughout the year. Even by the early seventeenth century London was becoming noted for its range of shops. Tea, coffee, sugar, tobacco, silks, porcelain and a vast variety of rare and luxurious goods from all over the world were displayed for purchase. This again was a source of cultural diffusion, as visitors returning home came to expect the provision of similar amenities in their own neighbourhoods.

## b) Leisure Towns

By the 1660s the fashion among the elites and middle orders for pleasure and relaxation resulted in the appearance of leisure towns all over England. Some focused on a particular attraction; Bath and Harrogate were spa towns, while Newmarket and Beverley catered for the growing passion for horse racing. Others, such as Northampton and Shrewsbury, provided a range of sophisticated amenities for the local elites. Some leisure towns, like Bath, Shrewsbury or Beverley, developed recreational facilities to replace declining economic activity. This supports the view that such towns were using leisure as a response to local needs to recreate employment. Evidence of this trend is to be found in the rising number of the wealthier townsmen being listed in occupations such as clockmaker, surveyor, gardener, confectioner, bookseller, milliner or snuff merchant. The erection of public buildings, such as assembly rooms or lending libraries, as well as the building or modernising of houses provided a valuable source of employment for the lower orders. Provincial capitals, like Norwich, Newcastle or Bristol, and county towns also catered for local recreational needs alongside their other economic activities. Even the newer towns, like Birmingham and Liverpool, had begun to cater for recreation and to build squares surrounded by fashionable houses by 1700.

Towns had become social centres for the county elites. Some, like Bath and Harrogate, had their own seasons which attracted fashionable society from all over the country. Many of the elites bought town houses in which they stayed with their families during the winter to avoid the rigours of the countryside. This trend created local seasons in most sizeable towns enabling the county landowners and the pseudo-gentry and their families to meet relatives and friends. While the men conducted business and exchanged news in the coffee houses, their wives and daughters made social calls and went shopping. During the summer local events such as the assize courts, horse races and fox hunts gave the elites the opportunity to meet socially.

The elites had become a valuable source of urban revenue. It was clearly in the interest of town authorities to provide amenities in order to encourage them to stay as long as possible. Streets were widened, paved and kept clean. Many authorities began to provide oil lamps for street lighting. Pumping works were built by rivers to supply towns with water through pipes and conduits. Often the process of modernisation was helped by the high incidence of town fires, such as the 'great fire' of Warwick in 1694, which enabled extensive re-building to be carried out. Many new stone, brick and tiled houses were built in the classical style, although often just a facade was added to older houses to save costs. Assembly rooms were built for dances, tea drinking, playing cards and other social activities. Lending libraries were opened and public parks with gravelled or paved walks, lawns, flower beds, shrubberies and glasshouses were created.

Apart from public amenities, a wide variety of shops, such as grocers, tobacconists, barbers, perfumers and confectioners opened. These supplied a large number of the exotic and luxury goods to be found in London. Smaller ale houses and inns were often converted to coffee shops to meet the new fashion. Larger coaching inns also became centres of business and entertainment. Inn keepers frequently staged musical evenings, dances, boxing matches and other shows to attract custom. In this way many towns became important focal points for local society. However, by no means all towns introduced improvements and new facilities. This is why the concept of a seventeenth-century 'urban renaissance' (suggesting the establishment of a national urban culture) has now been questioned.

## 3 Rationality, Progress and the Scientific Revolution

There is still considerable debate about the nature of the seventeenth-century scientific revolution. It is seen as ushering in a new rational approach to the study of science and nature, and to have introduced a confident and progressive view of mankind's ability to understand the universe. However, there is some dispute about whether this marked an entirely fresh approach. Some historians argue that it was a much more evolutionary process which continued to embody traditional ideas. This is also part of another debate about whether scientific and technological advances were achieved by sudden break-throughs by academic intellectuals or through the accumulative effect of minor improvements made by craftsmen and artisans.

### a) Progress and Co-operation

Until the seventeenth century science had been governed by scholastic and humanistic thinking. Science was largely derived from the classical Greeks, especially Aristotle, who used theoretical reasoning and logical deduction rather than observation and experiment. All knowledge was seen as revealed truth and as such was finite. This meant that it was thought that everything that there was to know about science had already been written, and that there was no need to try to make new discoveries. Scholars merely had to read the accepted authorities and did not need to observe or experiment. The outlook was pessimistic in that it was felt to be impossible to gain a greater knowledge of, or make any improvement to, the world. At the same time much of the existing scientific knowledge was intermingled with the occult (supernatural) and magic. All parts of the universe were thought to have souls, and natural phenomena were considered to have been caused by supernatural forces.

The Renaissance brought a growing belief in man's capacity for infinite knowledge. However, humanistic scholars adopted a neo-platonic philosophy. This was based on the writings of Plato combined with Oriental mysticism, and continued to mingle existing scientific knowledge with the occult. At the same time humanistic individualism did not encourage co-operation. Moreover, although there were scientific discoveries in the sixteenth century they were not backed by systematic research, mathematical quantitative investigation, or any knowledge of universal laws. As a result, although there was more optimism about man's ability to improve the world, it was clouded by a pessimistic feeling that the universe was controlled by the unknown forces of the occult.

The great change in the seventeenth century was the optimistic belief that human progress and knowledge had no boundaries. Rationality was replacing superstition, and the universe was seen as a physical entity that was governed by scientific laws which could be measured and analysed. The English scholar and politician, Francis Bacon, is considered to have been a major originator of this new approach. He was opposed to both scholasticism and humanism. In books such as *Advancement of Learning* (1605) he advocated scientific co-operation, whereby scholars worked together and shared ideas. Herein lay the idea of progress, with generations of scientists steadily adding to the body of human knowledge - a process that was never complete. At the same time, he recognised the need for methodical scientific research. This became the basis of empirical investigation, whereby no fact or theory could be accepted until it had been proved by observation and exhaustive experiment. In *Nova Atlantis* (1627) he visualised an ideal state ruled by scientists working together in laboratories for the benefit of mankind.

## b) Seventeenth-Century Scientific and Technological Progress

There are still doubts about the extent to which scientific objectivity actually existed in Stuart England. It has been pointed out that Bacon himself made no important discoveries and that his writings contained many untested scientific myths and errors. Although there were important advances, many of the leading English scholars were still fascinated by mysticism and the occult. At the same time, it is thought that most of the major technological break-throughs were based more on the painstaking work of craftsmen than on the insights of elite academics.

Isaac Newton was one of the key figures in the seventeenth-century English scientific revolution. His discovery of gravity and establishment of universal mechanical laws which governed the movement of all objects in the universe through forces of repulsion and attraction, was finally published in *Principia* (1687). Furthermore, his work on light and colour published in *Optics* (1704) firmly established him as the leading scientist of the period. His theories were exhaustively discussed by fellow members of the Royal Society, and in this respect he demonstrates the new spirit of co-operation. At the same time, Newton exhibits the ambivalence of Stuart science in that he retained a great interest in the occult and, like the medieval alchemists, believed that it should be possible to turn lead into gold. John Napier is another example of the continuing interest in pseudo-science. He made remarkable mathematical break-throughs in the development of the slide rule, decimal notation and logarithms. However he was very interested in astrology, and much of his mathematical work was designed to help him solve what he took to be a number code in the Book of Revelations.

Even so, the late seventeenth century was a great period of English scientific achievement. Apart from the work of Newton and Napier, a surprising number of important discoveries were made. William Harvey, court physician to Charles I, carried out anatomical research and published his theory of the circulation of the blood in 1628. Robert Hooke in *Miccrographia* (1664) revolutionised thinking in physics, astronomy and biology through his new law on elasticity. He also worked alongside Robert Boyle on his chemical experiments, and designed an air pump for Boyle's experiments into atmospheric pressure. At the same time, William Oughtred, the mathematician, made considerable advances in the development of trigonometry.

The Royal Society was founded specifically for 'the promotion of physico-mathematical experimental learning'. In addition, the government hoped that its members would investigate and solve technical problems, especially in navigation and mining. The Society was an excellent forum for scientific debate. However, its discussions were often acrimonious and exhibited controversy and rivalry rather than co-operation. Consequently, it did little to achieve any major technological advances. For example, Christopher Wren's study of submarine navigation, and William Petty's design of a two-keeled ship were of no practical use.

In fact, most of the technical improvements that were made came from the work of craftsmen. As early as 1600, William Gilbert, in *De Magnete,* acknowledged that much of his work on magnetism and navigation was based on the advice of craftsmen. The advances that were made were generally the result of delicate and painstaking workmanship. The new pendulum clock reduced daily error to one tenth of a second. Measuring scales were refined to weigh one five-hundredth of a grain. The art of lens grinding was vastly improved, and so enabled production of more efficient microscopes and telescopes. It was advances of this nature that enabled the major scientific discoveries of the period to be made.

Even though this was a highly formative scientific period there are still some doubts whether true empiricism and rationality had been established by the early eighteenth century. Although a new scientific synthesis was beginning to emerge it was still intermingled with neo-platonic ideas and mysticism. This has led to the suggestion that the process was more evolutionary than revolutionary. Scientists were still working within the old framework of belief, but they were developing a fresh conception of the world around them which led them to a different interpretation. More people were acknowledging that the universe was governed by mechanical forces rather than by magic and the supernatural. Objectivity and logical rationalisation were replacing subjectivity, and an optimistic belief in mankind's ultimate ability to master and understand the universe had emerged. This was the legacy of progress that was developed as the Enlightenment in the eighteenth century.

## 4 The Separation of Patrician and Popular Cultures?

The evidence for a marked cultural separation by the elites and middle orders from the lower orders is still conflicting and controversial. Many elements of oral culture and recreation persisted well into the nineteenth century and, certainly up to 1700, were shared by all sections of society. The major cultural divide appears to have been between those who could read and write and those who could not. Illiteracy became associated with the poor, so that even the literate among the lower orders came to scorn the illiterate 'rabble'.

## a) Traditional Oral Culture

Oral culture was based on an escapist belief in a supernatural fantasy world that was inhabited by goblins, fairies, witches, sorcerers, vampires and werewolves. It also incorporated a superstitious fear of nature and natural forces. Until the end of the Middle Ages all sections of lay society shared these beliefs. Such ideas had been undermined among the elites by increasing male lay literacy, and by the growth of rationality resulting from the Reformation, the Renaissance and the scientific revolution.

Before the Reformation it was generally believed that supernatural dangers and natural disasters threatening the community could be warded off by the ceremonies and magic of the medieval Church. Protestantism, with its condemnation of rituals and the worship of images and saints, had removed this protection. It has been suggested that to some extent this strengthened popular culture and weakened the Church. Many of the lower orders lost interest in religion and turned to sorcerers, witches and other 'cunning people' for protection, and used their own rituals, dances, charms, cures, spells and magic to avert disaster. It was these ideas and practices that persisted among the illiterate in many parts of the countryside, although possibly less so in the towns and industrial areas. These people became the ungodly, dancing rabble who were looked down upon by the more educated and affluent members of society.

## b) The Influence of Literacy

With the growth of literacy many of these oral traditions passed into the realm of folk lore and were investigated and written about by scholars and antiquarians. Fairy stories and other aspects of popular culture also became the subject matter of the increasing number of children's books that were being published. At the same time there was a huge demand for popular literature from the literate lower orders. Sales of ballads, almanacs, chapbooks incorporating romances, fables, history, astrology, popular science, cures, recipes, good advice and sensational news increased rapidly after 1660. These were sold by peddlers and travelling chapmen at fairs and markets, and on street corners. It is estimated that some 40,000 almanacs costing 2s 6d each were being sold every year, and the Stationers Company listed over 3,000 ballad titles as having been published by 1709. Such a demand suggests that there must have been a greater degree of literacy among many sections of the lower orders than has often been suspected. At the same time popular literature helped to conserve many elements of traditional culture. It is suggested that this became the basis of a new literate plebeian culture retaining much of the old escapism and fantasy, which became established in towns and industrial areas during the eighteenth century.

## c) Recreation and Leisure

Leisure, sport and recreation were other aspects of lower-order culture. Traditionally these had been part of community activities that had centred around the ale house. Dancing, May Day celebrations, festivals, fairs, weddings, wakes, harvest suppers and village ales had been important events in village life breaking up the drudgery of work. They were augmented by sporting contests such as bowls, tennis, football, wrestling and athletics, and gambling on such things as cards, cock fighting, and boxing matches.

The Restoration marked the end of the imposition of Puritan morality during the Interregnum and ushered in a period of frivolity and laxity. This is seen as helping to promote popular sports and recreations, or at the very least, in slowing down their decline. Samuel Pepys commented that the return of Charles II was marked by the setting up of over 6,000 maypoles for dancing, marking a revival of popular sports, games and festivals. In any case, many of the leisure pursuits indulged in by the lower orders were enjoyed equally by the elites and middle orders. They both organised and participated in many sporting contests, they

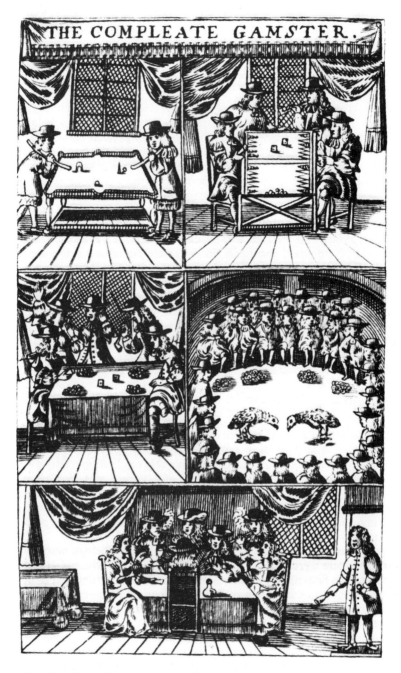

*The Compleate Gamster (1680 edition)*

frequented the ale houses, and drinking and gambling were just as much a passion among the elites as they were among the lower orders. Horse racing at Newmarket or Epsom became just as popular with the lower orders as it was with the elites. Moreover, the growth of entertainment, ease of travel and the availability of cheap alcohol and tobacco encouraged the pursuit of leisure among the lower orders despite government criticism.

## d) A Separation of Cultures?

Superstition and traditional thinking persisted among the academic intelligentsia. This suggests that despite the growth in rational thinking there was not an unbridgeable cultural gulf between even the scientific scholar and the illiterate poor. Furthermore, a shared interest and participation throughout society in recreational and sporting activities tended to restrict any gap that was being created. As yet there was no rigid divide between the urban and rural populations, with large numbers of urban workers going out into the countryside every year to help with the harvesting and join the rural festivals. Equally, it is evident that social and cultural differences were developing at various levels. Among the lower orders an oral popular culture existed alongside a literate plebeian culture. There were increasing differences between closed agricultural and the open industrial parishes. Ease of travel, urban expansion and government intervention were undermining the traditional rural community. Evidence from various parts of the country shows that the lower-middling groups were anxious to disassociate themselves from what they saw as the disorderly mob. Village constables and other 'worthies' were becoming increasingly likely to close ale houses and to bring poachers and the disorderly before the local magistrates.

Yet, despite growing differences, it is difficult to say that real cultural separation had occurred by 1700. Traditional elements remained at all levels of society. As with so many aspects of Stuart England, continuity was more evident than change.

## 5 Conclusion

Although there were significant cultural changes at all levels of society, they were taking place within a context of considerable underlying continuity. A national framework was beginning to be created through government political and economic centralisation and improved travel facilities, but provincial and local independence still remained. Although the growing influence of London had not yet established a distinctive urban culture, many provincial towns were beginning to develop into quite sophisticated leisure centres along the lines established in the capital. Even so, England remained predominantly rural, and county communities retained their own distinctive social and cultural characteristics.

One of the great achievements of late Stuart culture was the considerable advances in science. However, although Newton, Napier, Boyle and other members of the Royal Society made highly important discoveries, it is now doubted whether this marked such a clean break with the past. Even among the progressive scientific intellectuals the new vision of a universe governed by mechanical laws was still clouded by remnants of traditional thinking.

There is still a great deal of debate over the extent to which there was a clear separation between the new progressive, optimistic rationality of the elites, and the traditional, oral, escapist popular culture of the lower orders. The issue is clouded by the growth of lower-order male literacy and the resultant high demand for popular literature. This is thought, by preserving oral traditions, to have strengthened popular culture. Even so it is agreed that there was a cultural separation taking place between the illiterate masses and the rest of society.

It has been suggested that an important aspect of Stuart cultural change was that it was being used to maintain the social hierarchy. Social differentiation was being retained through an emphasis on display and lifestyles. The fashionable elites adopted a pose of languid, worldly superficiality to distinguish themselves from what they saw as the worthy, but dull, middle orders. The middle orders, while emulating some of the characteristics of the elites, disapproved of their extravagance and excesses. To counteract this they assumed a lifestyle of propriety and respectability which set them apart from both the elites and the unruly mob.

---

## Making notes on 'Cultural Change'

The first section looks at the controversies over the influence of London and the court, the scientific revolution and the possible divergence between patrician and popular culture. These are fundamental issues: it is essential to make careful notes on the key points of the debate. Section 2 examines to what extent London was creating a national urban culture. You should decide whether there was an 'urban renaissance', and how far the provinces and the county communities were retaining their individuality. The next section assesses the impact of the scientific revolution. You need to consider very carefully whether late Stuart society was truly rational, optimistic and progressive, and to what extent it was still influenced by traditional thinking. The final section looks at the controversy over the possible separation of patrician and popular culture. You need to consider the extent of any separation, and whether culture and lifestyle were becoming an expression of social position.

These are difficult issues and you should make very careful notes, and refer to your notes on chapter 5, before coming to any decision.

---

*Answering essay questions on 'Cultural Change'*

As examiners tend to concentrate on topics over which there has been some disagreement among historians, you will be well advised to prepare yourself to answer questions on the three controversial issues covered by this chapter: i) the influence of London and the court, ii) the scientific revolution, and, iii) the possible divergence between patrician and popular culture. Study the following questions:

1  'By 1700 the influence of London was all pervasive in the elite cultural life of England.' Discuss.
2  Was there a scientific revolution in seventeenth-century England?
3  To what extent did England lose its cultural unity during the seventeenth century?
4  Why did London dominate the cultural life of Stuart England?
5  Do you agree that 'the term "scientific revolution" is a misnomer when applied to seventeenth-century England'?
6  Did the events of the Stuart period strengthen or weaken popular culture in England?

One of the stages that you should routinely go through when thinking about how to tackle an essay title is to scrutinise the wording of the question to identify any assumptions that may need to be challenged, or at least to be discussed. This stage will be particularly important with two of the questions above. Which two questions? Sometimes the discussion of assumptions will comprise a major part of your answer. This is the case with question 4. What is the assumption that will need considerable discussion in this question?

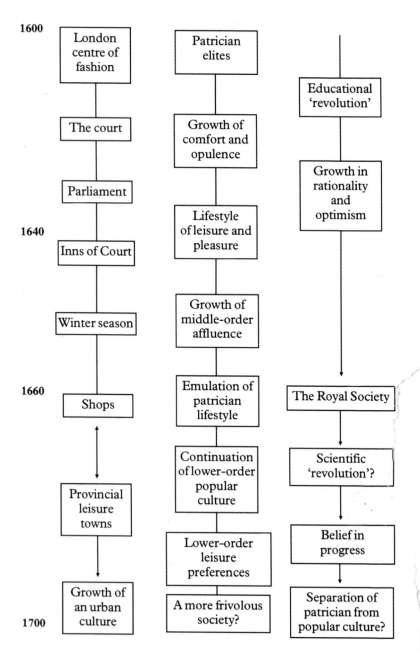

*Summary - Cultural Change*

# Further Reading

The controversy over the English Civil War and the variety of approaches now being used to interpret the economy and society have generated a very wide range of general and specialist books on Stuart England. Chapter 1 discusses the historiography of these debates and cites some of the major contributions to them, and other leading authorities are mentioned in subsequent chapters. The following selection (mainly not cited elsewhere in the book) suggests some of the general books written from differing perspectives which will help you to reach an overview of the period, and lists a few specialist works to illustrate the complexities of the historical debate

**B. Coward,** *Social Change and Continuity in Early Modern England 1550-1750* (Longman, 1988) provides a full and straightforward account of the Stuart economy and society and has a useful bibliography.

**K. Wrightson,** *English Society 1580-1680,* (Hutchinson, 1982) is an excellent and accessible account of English society that is particularly useful for studying the non-elite sections of society.

**C. Hill,** A *Century of Revolution 1603-1714,* (2nd ed. Nelson, 1980) is still a very popular and controversial Marxist analysis of the period.

**M. Prior,** (ed.) *Women in English Society 1500-1800* (Methuen, 1985) and **A. Fraser,** *The Weaker Vessel,* (Weidenfeld and Nicolson, 1984) provide good examples of differing approaches to women's history.

**C. Coleman,** *The Economy of England 1450-1750* (OUP, 1977) is still a comprehensive and uncomplicated account of the Stuart economy.

**C.G.A. Clay,** *Economic Expansion and Social Change 1500-1750,* (CUP, 1984), **J. Thirsk,** *Economic Policy and Projects,* (Clarendon Press, 1978) and **F. Fisher,** *London and the English Economy 1500-1700,* (Hambledon, 1988) offer valuable alternative economic perspectives.

**R.A. Houston,** *The Population History of Britain and Ireland 1500-1750,* (Macmillan, 1992) provides a shorter and more accessible alternative to the definitive work of E.A. Wrigley and R.S. Schofield.

**S. Easton,** *Disorder and Discipline: Popular Culture from 1550 to the Present* (Temple Smith, 1988) and **T. Harris,** (ed), *Popular Culture in England c. 1500-1850* (Macmillan, 1993) offer contrasting views on popular culture.

**I. Wallerstein,** *The Modern World-System,* Vols I and II, (Academic Press, 1974) and **A.K. Smith,** *Creating a World Economy: Merchant Capital, Colonialism and World Trade, 1400-1825,* (Westview Press, 1991) offer interesting alternative views of the world economy.

# Index